Dr. Darcy Lord

52 WEEKS OF RELIEF

Uplifting Provocations
for Stress Reduction
and Self-Care

Relief Room Publishing
52 Weeks of Relief - First Edition Trade Book, 2019
Dr. Darcy Lord

Editorial Review: Betty Lapp, Theresa Gianquinto and Sherm Stratton
Cover and Interior Book Design: Jackson Design
diane.jackson5@icloud.com

Published in the United States by Relief Room Publishing
ISBN: 978-1-7337225-8-2
Library of Congress Control Number: 2019902984

To order additional books: amazon.com

Or, visit the website at: drdarcylord.com

E-book also available

To the deep essence of Divine Intelligence
within each one of us that forever knows
and loves our beauty, our worth, our strength,
and our infinite goodness; and continually
calls us back toward the relief and well-being
of living our highest good.

Acknowledgements

There are so many beautiful individuals who have blessed and made richer and happier my life; and because the writings within come from the "stuff" of my life, they have all in some way assisted in the completion of this book. While I won't be able to thank personally everyone who has touched my heart—and therefore added depth and richness to this book—my deep, deep gratitude moves out toward every one of you who has blessed me with your Beingness.

I extend enormous gratitude, love, and thanks to: My wonderful son, Nikolas. Thank you for deciding to come and be my son this lifetime! You are a blessing to me in a million ways and your laughter, questions, brightness, and enormous heart have often been the stuff from which my writing comes! I love you so very much and I am so proud of who you are.

The awesome employees of Sarasota County Government (SCG), to whom I have written many "Stress Blurbs." I have never in all my years speaking and training experienced a more beautiful group of people as a whole than you guys. Your true desire to serve; to do well; to take care of others; to be ethical, kind, and hard-working; and your commitment to being great humans amazes and inspires me. Many of you have become my wonderful friends and I love you all more than you know. For all of you at SCG on my "Stress Blurb list" and in my many classes, thank you for your constant encouragement to write and be myself!

My friends—near and far—who love and support me, and who play with me in the things of spirituality, consciousness, opening the heart, laughter, meditation, the mind-body-spirit connection, and well-being generally: Chris Murphy, Julia Dennis, Angela Deem, Polly Pitchford, Heidi Kaplan, Mary McCarthy-Hageman, Margaux Surette, Dee Harmer, Dr. Maryanna Klatt, and my Unity of Venice gang. So much of my life work comes out of our discussions and gatherings and laughter and love. I don't have words to thank you enough for being who you are and for being in my life. I love you dearly.

The many mentors and teachers over the years who have made such a huge and wonderful difference in my life and therefore have positively affected and directly influenced my speaking and writing: Louis Hay, Dr. Wayne W. Dyer, Ernest Holmes, Jack Canfield, Esther and Jerry Hicks, Dr. Deepak Chopra, Dr. Jon Kabat-Zinn, Florence Scovel-Shinn, Rev. Patricia Reiter and Rev. Robin Reiter, Alan Cohen, Rev. Dr. Michael Beckwith, Shawn Achor, Dr. Rollin McCraty and the whole HeartMath team, Sanaya Roman, Neale Donald Walsch, Steve Harrison, James Malinchak, Thich Nhat Hanh, John C. Maxwell, Bob and Carol Gilbert, Rev. Dr. Dennis and Ruth Kenny, and John and Nancy Hampson. Thank you for your courage to be who you truly are and for writing, speaking, teaching, and creating that which you do. Your lightness of being is a radiant thing and you all uplift me!

My wonderful mom, Betty Lapp. Thank you for your infinite patience and support reading, editing, and encouraging me to get this book completed. I can't tell you thank you enough for always being proud of me, always being willing to hear me read to you yet another part of the book, always telling me you are blessed or uplifted from my work, and for always knowing my potential. I am so thankful that you are my mom and my friend.

Denise Murphy, my sweet "seester." Thank you for continually being there to help me find the right word, for laughing with me, and for always letting me feel however I feel, whether that's peaceful, happy, powerful, and big; or scared, tired, frustrated, or impatient. I'm so glad we came to be on this planet together as sisters!

Diane Jackson, artist, graphic designer and earth angel. With extraordinary amounts of patience, gentleness, and competence you turned my words into a beautiful book, and always you remind me about my own light and radiance! Huge love and gratitude!

Theresa Gianquinto (Mama T), editor and friend extraordinaire. Thank you for saying yes!

And finally, my students, clients, and audiences everywhere. I am truly honored by your time and energy, your insights, your commitment to well-being and personal growth, and your trust in me. Thank you for letting me explore and create with you, speak and write to you, develop curriculum and programs for you, facilitate trainings and workshops because of you, meditate with you, and experience relief with you. You are the reason I do what I do and without you this book would only be a shell of what it is. Thank you!

Contents

Introduction

If you find yourself reading these words, or any of the weekly provocations within, then this book is for you. You—exactly as you are in this moment—with your stresses, worries, and tiredness, but also with your strength, courage, and capabilities. The fifty-two "Stress Blurbs" as I like to call them, which make up *52 Weeks of Relief*, are for you right here and right now.

I am sure of two things. First, that Life is good and is *always* for us. And second, that relief is possible this very moment *even before things have changed.* Depending on where you are today relief may show up as even greater happiness, fullness, or satisfaction with your life. Or it could show up as worry subsiding just long enough so that you can breathe; sleeping *even one time* through the night; finding respite, peace, or surrender in a really difficult situation; or simply experiencing hope that things can get better.

As you read and play in the ideas of this book, relief will likely move through you differently on different days. Sometimes you may feel passion, inspiration, or motivation to reach higher and move forward more intentionally. Other days you may be reminded to simply bask in the awesome power of non-doing, playing, or turning kindness upon yourself.

Use the guidance of your own being to know how to use the individual chapters. They were designed to give you fifty-two weeks—one full year—of gentle guidance and support to see and do things differently, in order that your stress would begin to soften and your well-being would continue to expand.

My suggestion is that you read through the entire book first, allowing the ideas and perspectives to wash through your whole being—your heart, your mind, your emotions, and even your physiology. After that, begin to utilize the provocations in any way you want. You may want to start with number one, putting that exercise to use for a full week, then move on to number two, and so on until you make your way through a year engaging in all of the practices. You may instead just close your eyes and flip to see which one you open to by "chance." Or, you may want to read through the chapter titles and turn to the one that calls to you in the moment. Of course, it's really about you choosing the way that works best for you.

No matter how you do it, know that the intent is for you to move through the chapters in such a way that you come out the other side having benefitted from the ideas written here because they have in some way *called you back to your own highest good.* I happen to believe that is not only possible, but probable, as I like to think that you have made your way to this book, and this book to you, by divine appointment. There is something wonderful and strong in that!

I wish for you great love and great happiness. I wish for you beautiful relationships, and deep meaning and purpose in your life. I wish for you good health and effortless prosperity. And mostly I wish for you *Relief* in ways that reduce your stress, strengthen your resiliency, remind you of your innate goodness, and uplift you to the very core of your Being.

Positive change
is possible,
healing is possible,
love is possible.

Week 1

Life is Good and is Always for Us

I know I can be Pollyanna. I like that about me. I like that it feels true to the very core of my being that good is possible, positive change is possible, healing is possible, love is possible. In all situations, at all junctures, good *is.* I know we don't always act on it and I know that many people are hurting. I do know that. And at the same time the possibility to experience good at any moment, on many different levels, is always present.

I think it might be true that out of all the things I like to write and talk about, all the things I try to live in my own life and help others remember, this one may be the most important to me: the fact that Life is good and is always *for* us. Always. Even when it feels not true or possible. That's the thing that I want so much for everyone to believe, feel, remember. Because when we remember that, when down deep somewhere we really know that, when we trust that Life is *for* us and never against us, it's so much easier to remember our own magnificence. It's so much more possible to live our greatest version of ourselves. It's so much more natural to come back to, and live from, our highest possibility. And isn't that always the point?

Albert Einstein was brilliant by most anyone's standards. Someone once told me that Mr. Einstein said the most important question worth asking about was if the Universe was benevolent. Was it good and

I think we would behave differently if we really believed at the core of our beings that life cared about us and wanted our highest and best.

kind? And his answer was, "Yes, it is." I will always be in Albert's camp. With a passion. I want us all to be able to feel the respite, relief, and grand possibility that comes from believing—no, from knowing and *feeling* at a deep level—that Life or the Universal Essence or God is always and forever *for* us; that we are inherently good, worthy, and loved; that we are guided every day all day toward living a beautiful life, toward creating a world that works for everyone.

I think we would behave differently if we really believed at the core of our beings that Life cared about us and wanted our highest and best. We would breathe easier and sleep easier. We would more often hear the quiet guidance that says all sorts of things like, "Let it go," "Who cares if others don't approve?" "Stop (or start) working now," "Forgive yourself," "It's time to move on," "Is it working for you?" "Let them off the hook," "This job doesn't serve you anymore," "You are allowed to be happy," and on and on.

If we trusted that Life was good and that it was *for* us I bet we wouldn't push so hard and keep doing things that weren't working. And I think we would have a different perspective when things seemed to go wrong. We might simply breathe and shift our perception, or be more nurturing with ourselves, or go in a different direction, or be more compassionate with others, or understand how strong we really are.

Even if it's a stretch, here is your provocation for the week. Practice seeing yourself and your world through eyes and a heart that believe, "Life is good and is *always* for me." I have found that it's a choice more than a static belief really. Whether "good" or "bad" things happen to you (and around the world) this week, attempt to reframe your judgment about it through a lens that sees

Pretend that you could assume that Life is good, that it is for you, that it wants everyone's happiest and best, and that it loves and approves of you always.

and feels compassion and love coming ever toward you and ever toward everyone else too. Pretend you could assume that Life is good, that it is *for* you, that it wants everyone's happiest and best, and that it loves and approves of you always. After a few days you may be wonderfully surprised at how easily you can breathe! Life *is* good and it is *for* us. It is *for* you. Always.

I think you may be
wonderfully surprised to see
just how many people are
living with integrity and honor,
guided by higher principles, and
loving freely and openly.

Week 2

The Real News

I rarely watch the news. I particularly avoid it anywhere near bedtime. Dr. Wayne Dyer used to say that whatever is in our consciousness right before we go to bed "marinates" there all night long. When I think of a typical news broadcast, it's not what I want to marinate my thoughts, feelings, and consciousness in all night long. I have found something interesting about the news however. It's "News" because it's *newsworthy,* right? I think of newsworthy as relating to things that are new, different, exciting, timely, need to know—i.e. *not commonplace.* This is a little weird, but follow me here: because the situations and stories in the news are usually negative, and *aren't* commonplace, it means that much of what is going on in the world which is commonplace is often positive and life affirming, or at worst, mundane and neutral. *That's* the real news. Here are a few examples:

For every person or group of people on the News committing hate crimes or acts of terror, how many other groups of people are living out their days with kindness and inner strength; with respect for diversity; being socially responsible; hoping for, or actively working toward, peace, prosperity, compassion, and respect for all people?

For every mom on the News who abandoned or killed her child, how many moms are on the planet right now who are loving, responsible, committed, and truly want the best for their children, even if they *are* often exhausted and impatient?

What we look
for expands.

For every political leader or government entity on the News who cares more about money and power than all else, how many public servants at local, state, and national levels are attempting to serve the public in the best way they can, with high degrees of integrity and decency?

For every gang member on the News who has turned to drugs and violence, how many young people go to school most days (even if they *are* bored with it), volunteer their time somewhere, act with courage when someone needs help, follow their parents' rules (at least mostly), help out with finances or siblings, and truly want to make a positive difference?

For every man on the News who has raped or beaten a woman, how many men go through their days respectfully, responsibly, honorably, and with an attempt to live up to personal commitments, financial obligations, others' expectations, and most of society's rules?

For every organization on the News whose leaders care only about profit, even at the expense of others, how many professionals are actively attempting to run a legitimate business in such a manner as to create a win-win situation for everyone?

Here's your provocation for the week, whether you watch the news or just hear about it from other people. Whatever is the negative, newsworthy situation, make a strong, active attempt to find 5-10 situations or people *anywhere* who are doing the opposite. I think you may be wonderfully surprised to see just how many people are living with integrity and honor, guided by higher principles, and loving freely and openly.

What we look for expands. Until there are shows that air the "Real News," let's all keep looking out for it anyway.

I want us to feel
the preciousness of
our own selves.

Week 3

Loving Ourselves

Babies love themselves—totally, completely, hilariously. Little kids love themselves—with messiness and chaos, and without embarrassment. Most grown-ups? Not so much. I don't know when that happens exactly, but I want us to change it. I want us to feel the preciousness of our own selves. I want us to see our own beauty, our own great talents and gifts. I want us to revel in the fact that our hearts are wonderful, bright, and loving—even when we are overdone. I want us each to appreciate the fact that we get hurt, sad, angry, frustrated, scared, and overwhelmed—but that we keep bouncing back from it day after day. It's amazing actually.

Even on our worst, most stress-filled days, most of us still have moments when we're simply kind to others. It's a beautiful thing. What if we turned some of that back on ourselves? What if today, and all this week, you turned kindness back onto yourself? What would it look like, what would it *feel* like, if you decided to be sincerely kind to you? How could you show yourself today that you love you? Even if it feels silly or uncomfortable, even if it feels not true, even if you have to pretend—try anyway. Ask yourself, "If I were going to be kind to me today, if I were going to take actions (or non-actions!) that showed I loved myself, what would my day look like?"

Would you be more patient with you? Or criticize yourself less? Would you release procrastination and do something you have been meaning to do? Or give yourself a break when you didn't? Would you appreciate your own values and strengths? Perhaps

If I were going to be
kind to me today,
if I were going to take
actions (or non-actions!)
that showed I loved myself,
what would my
day look like?

use them even more this week? Would you go at a pace that feels good? Or eat things that make you feel good? Or choose to be around people who make you feel good? Would you do something that made you proud of you? Or maybe just be proud of who you are for making it through times that have been difficult? Would you choose to believe in yourself? What else?

Here is your provocation for the week. Ask yourself the above questions and take note as answers start to emerge. You may be pleasantly surprised at what you find. Also, try this beautiful activity: press both of your hands over your heart—firmly enough to feel the warmth coming from your hands; gently enough to give yourself the message that this is about treating you with loving care. Stay there for a few long breaths. Then close your eyes and ask inwardly, "If I chose to treat myself lovingly right now, what is it that I most need?"

Even the simple question is enough to have internal shifts begin. And as a spoiler alert—it turns out that when we start loving ourselves, it's *really* good news for everyone around us too! Try it this week and see what happens.

We are simply not
mean to one another, or
abusive in any way, when
we ourselves feel
at our best.

Week 4

Mean People

There are two bumper stickers I really like. One says, "Visualize whirled peas." That's just hilarious. I saw it when I was first learning about consciously creating our experiences through visualization and the Law of Attraction, and it's a take-off of the "Visualize World Peace" bumper sticker (which I love too). Another one that I particularly like says, "Mean People Suck," mostly because it just makes me laugh. And because I like when people are nice. I do. I like when we are kind to one another. Somehow it doesn't seem like it should be that hard to do. Until I remember times when I have been mean—then it makes more sense.

I never plan to be mean. That would feel awful. As I look back at times when I have been mean I notice two things. The first is that I am normally only mean to the people I am closest to… like family or good friends that I love. How weird and sad is that? The second thing I notice is that I am only "mean" (read "impatient, judgmental, harsh, critical, rigid, condescending," etc.) when I am feeling out of sorts or simply *not* happy and well myself. Often it's when I am physically tired and feeling "pressed" to do more than I can easily get done. Other times it's when I am experiencing a deeper level of fear, worry, sadness, or difficulty that I don't know how to "fix."

I guess that's not rocket science, but for me it was good to remember that we are simply not mean to one another, or abusive in any way, when we ourselves feel at our best—whether that means feeling safe, strong,

When we take good care of
ourselves we are much more
able to serve others
in positive, empowered,
and authentic ways.

peaceful, happy, fulfilled, or like our needs are met. In a way, that is another big call for taking our own personal responsibility to engage in stress reduction and self-care. Because when we take good care of ourselves we are much more able to serve others in positive, empowered, and authentic ways.

But even more than that, it's a call for compassion. Here is your provocation for the week. Whenever you experience someone being "mean," take a minute to ask yourself, "What might be going on that could make her or him act like that?" Then actually take the time to make up a story. Perhaps she has a sick elderly dad and is exhausted emotionally and physically because the rest of the family isn't helping out; maybe he is so far in debt that he has lost all hope of relief and is trying to hide it from his family; perhaps she is worried about her children who are making unhealthy choices in relationships, or using drugs and alcohol to deal with their new responsibilities; maybe he just got in another fight with his spouse or girlfriend; perhaps she lost her job—again; maybe he learned that he has cancer or diabetes; maybe she is running late to work and is scared of being treated badly by the boss or co-workers; maybe he always feels criticized and finally just doesn't care anymore. The list can go on and on.

And then, if you happen to find someone who seems to be *chronically* mean, ask yourself, "To turn out like that what *might* their childhood have looked like? What *might* their life in general have been like up until now?" Of course, we will never really know, but I have found that this exercise helps me soften, both toward others and toward myself, when I practice it. In some ways we are way stronger than we think we are. But in other ways we are way more vulnerable and sensitive than we think

By attempting to
take the high road
of compassion and
acceptance, we help
soften and ease not only
others' difficulties but
our own as well.

we "should" be. By attempting to take the high road of compassion and acceptance, even when difficult, I feel sure that we help soften and ease not only others' difficulties but our own as well. How's that for a win-win situation?

When I pretend that
I have one more
beautiful day to live,
the things that have been
feeling overwhelming
are not quite so
important anymore.

Week 5

When I Croak

I know it's politically incorrect to talk about this… but here goes. There is something I do sometimes and the impact on me is amazing. I pretend that I have croaked, expired, died, left my body, whatever you want to call it. And then I pretend that I get to come back for another day—today. I think if I remembered to live like that *every day*, my life would be very different. And way better than it already is now.

Here are a few things that happened the last time I did it. I felt the wind on my face—really felt it—and it was amazing. The sun made my hair warm on top. Delicious! I saw pink flowers growing on the gangly bushes in the front of a building I was passing by and they were more beautiful and intricate than I had ever noticed. Then I kept thinking how lucky I was that I get to go pick up my son, Nikolas, from school and hug him. I get to smile and look people right in the eyes as I pass; and I get to call my mom and make her laugh at me for being dorky.

I'm not making light of all the things that stress us out or make us feel overwhelmed. I know they are real. But when I pretend that I have one more beautiful day to live—here on the planet with things just as they are right now—the things that have been feeling overwhelming are not quite so important any more. At least not in the moment when I am feeling really grateful to still be in this marvelous body, with these amazing thoughts and feelings, beautiful heart, and perhaps most importantly, with all of the awesome people I have around me.

Because you are worth it!

Here is your provocation this week if you choose to play in it. See what truly matters to your heart by imagining one more day to live after you have already been gone. What might it be like to come back, to get to be here again with people, pets, experiences, and things? You may find that sometimes when you dwell on what matters to you, some of the many stresses can slide away, or at least lose some of their power. Try it this week and see what happens.

And remember to take good care of yourself today, because you are worth it!

I think we would
inspire people around us
without even trying.

Week 6

What if Today Really Mattered?

I was driving and caught myself in autopilot mode. Do you ever have those times? When you notice you are just going through the motions and everything is all just "fine." Then I had the thought, "I want this day to matter." And I felt myself come back from wherever I was—more present, more full, more here, more real. I don't know why that thought came to me, but it was beautiful.

What would happen for you if you decided to make today matter? What would your day look like? How would you be with your family? How would you be with people and projects at work? How would you be with mundane chores at home? Where would you choose to put your thoughts? What would you decide to focus on?

What if this very day *everyone* decided that today really mattered? Do you know what I think? I think our core values would come out. I think we would really look at the people we were with, and truly hear them. I think we would remember who means the most to us and call them, hug them, love them, send them a prayer or healing energy, or just remember to appreciate them.

I also think priorities would fall into place effortlessly. I think our courage and determination to do our best would come out; and our willingness to be easier with us and everyone else would show up. I think compassion and patience would emerge; as well as a tenacity and heightened intelligence to find ways to

I bet we would finally figure out how to engage both our minds and our hearts.
Amazing!

make things better for everyone. I think we would find a way to let go of habits that don't serve us, and find the strength and self-love to commit to our highest good. I think we would inspire people around us without even trying. I bet we would finally figure out how to engage *both* our minds *and* our hearts. Amazing!

What do you think might happen if globally we all remembered that today matters? Your provocation is twofold this week. First, dwell on what could happen if the whole world played this game. Second, decide right now that today really matters and live this week from that perspective.

I think the first person
we have to learn how
to forgive is
ourselves.

Week 7

The Difficult Art of Self-Forgiveness

I was thinking about forgiveness. Whether we practice it or not, most of us have heard of the importance and benefits of forgiving people. It's not about liking or condoning negative, abusive, or unhealthy behavior; it's simply about forgiving the person because it doesn't serve us (or anyone) to hold onto the hurt and judgment. Most counseling practices, spiritual traditions, universal philosophies, and personal growth processes eventually lead us back to the art of forgiving. But sometimes I think we go about it backwards. We always get taught to forgive other people. But I think the first person we have to learn how to forgive is ourselves. And I think that is even harder to do. Have you ever tried to forgive someone, or be kind, compassionate, or nurturing when you are really annoyed or irritated with yourself? I can't decide if it's more sad or comical.

For me it's as clear as this. When I am being hard on myself, I am harder on everyone else too—even if I pretty it up with politeness. When I don't let myself off the hook first, I am not able to let you off the hook either. However, when I decide to remember that I am good, in spite of my mess-ups, when I intend to do better next time, and when I work on forgiving myself and then making amends where needed, *then* beautiful things can happen.

So here is your provocation for the week. First, think of some things you have been disappointed in yourself

When I am being hard on myself, I am harder on everyone else too.

about, or have not forgiven yourself for, or wish you had done (or would do) differently.

Here are three of mine:

1. When I am impatient with Nikolas (my son)
2. When I procrastinate on my lifework projects
3. When I eat more sugar than feels right/good/ healthy for my body

Second, take those things and remember at least three times when you have done them differently and in a way that felt good, loving, healthy, or "right" for everyone involved. With my examples I could ask myself:

1. Have there been three specific times when I had infinite patience with Nikolas? (Oh yes!)
2. Are there three times when I have moved wonderfully on my writing and speaking projects? (Definitely!)
3. Have there been three times when I have treated my body in a way that makes me feel strong, healthy, and proud of me? (Of course!)

As you do this exercise, sense any gentleness or softening that begins to move through. Just breathe with that awareness and be willing to treat yourself kindly. Decide to remember all the ways and times that you have done well, and then choose consciously to let yourself off the hook for anything that has needed your love, compassion, understanding, and forgiveness. It's after we engage in our own gentle forgiveness that we can then extend that feeling to others in an authentic way, whether through making amends (if we perceive we have done something "wrong") or offering forgiveness (if we perceive they have done something "wrong").

Just breathe with that awareness and be willing to treat yourself kindly.

It's interesting (and beautiful), when I have used a mean or condescending voice with Nikolas and I say "I'm really sorry," he normally looks right at me and says, "That's okay." And I know he means it because I can feel it. I think he can mean it because he still feels good about himself. Which perhaps is why he can also say "I'm sorry" so easily. The next time you do something that you know was not your highest choice, imagine saying, "I wish I wouldn't have done it that way. I'm sorry." And then imagine the highest, most intelligent, and most loving part of you saying and truthfully meaning, "That's okay." What powerful and transforming moments can happen when we are willing to step into the difficult art of self-forgiveness.

It is about choosing to see
what is good, what is working,
and what is right in the world,
even when lots of people
have decided that nothing
good is happening.

Week 8

Personal Mission Statements

I wonder what would happen if we all created a personal mission statement for our lives. And then chose to remember it throughout the day, even at work or with our kids. I wonder if we would feel as frantic, stressed, worried, or bored. I wonder if we would still move through the days on autopilot as so many of us often do. What would your mission statement be about? Being the best parent you could be? Standing up for yourself and what you know to be good, true, and "right," even when others stand against you? Living each day loving people unconditionally? Helping people or animals? Using your creativity, skills, and talents to make the world a better place? Being at peace in every moment? Fulfilling your universal commitments? Living in spiritual oneness? Making a positive difference to people around you? Being an important role model by taking good care of yourself? Choosing kindness over being right? Deciding to always see the good and infinite possibilities in people even when they are not showing that to you? Living your highest vision?

It is still a work in progress but mine is definitely about living in such a way that people around me feel uplifted and empowered. It is about walking around on the planet as the highest version of me that I can. And about helping people remember that *we are good*—

It is about taking what
truly matters to your heart
and putting it into a
powerful statement of
how you want to live,
and move, and
have your being.

no matter what other messages we may have heard. It's about reminding myself, and everyone else, that life is good and is always FOR us. And it is about choosing to see what is good, what is working, and what is right in the world, even when lots of people have decided that nothing good is happening.

What might happen if we all turned our attention toward what calls to us from within—toward what really matters? That is what I think a personal mission statement helps us do. It is about taking what truly matters to your heart and putting it into a powerful statement of how you want to live, and move, and have your being. I do wonder what would happen. I think we would change the planet. I think we would heal it and ourselves in a million different, beautiful ways.

And that is your provocation for this week. Decide what is really important to you—and then write out your own personal mission statement. Here is a current working version of mine: *My intention is to experience my own joy and divine alignment enough to help uplift the consciousness of the planet as a best-selling author and speaker continually calling people back to their own highest good.* It feels awesome each time I focus on that. And there is a good chance you will feel wonderful simply by having worked on yours too!

What you are thinking about
is absolutely
up to you
moment by moment.

Week 9

Always My Choice

Remember the glass half-full vs. half-empty thing? I know it can sound Pollyanna, impractical, and sort of pointless at times. This week's provocation is probably more for me than it is for you… but here it is.

I had a family member visiting whom I had not seen for ten years. There is a list of what makes me crazy about her behaviors and attitudes. When I dwell on those things—because quite frankly up until this point it has been hard not to—I feel… well, yucky. I feel crunched up, squeezed up inside, somehow sticky or heavy or pressed on or drained or—just yucky. Those behaviors and attitudes that I have such a hard time with are real. They are factual. They actually happen. So I am not pretending that they do not.

However, those things that are annoying or challenging or difficult for me—I promise you—are only half of the story. Here is what is also true about that same person: her smile is beautiful and sweet and gentle and real. When she laughs you can't help laughing with her because it is so heartfelt and authentic. She was so kind, present, and wonderful with my son, Nikolas. She has so much integrity that I would trust her with anything. And perhaps most important, her heart is incredibly, beautifully open and loving toward everyone she is ever around. Truly. How different I feel when I remember those things. I feel myself soften and become more open, relaxed, and easy. And when I wrote that thing about her heart, a great big smile came across my face. All of that is because *our bodies, our emo-*

The empowerment
and relief you can feel
are simply amazing.

tions, and our stress levels respond immediately to what we are thinking about. And here is the magical, amazing, powerful part. It's not rocket science, but it's infinitely important to your well-being: what you are thinking about is absolutely up to you moment by moment! The same is true for all of us. It's unbelievably cool, actually. What you think about directly and immediately affects your stress levels, health, and general well-being. *And* what you think about is absolutely up to you and under your own direction. At least that's true *when you are aware* that you can direct or change your thoughts any time you want to. I am simply reminding you that *that is true.*

So here is your provocation for the week. When you become aware that you are feeling challenged, or tired, or frustrated, or hurting, or anxious, or impatient, or mad, or anything else that feels "not so good," understand that it is because *in that moment* you are focusing on, thinking about, or knowing what you are "against." In other words it is when you are noticing what you *do not* want or like. When that happens just allow yourself to be there, in that place of experiencing what you are "against" (i.e. my family member's attitude and actions) until it feels like you have had enough of it or until you are ready to shift your perspective. And *as soon as you are ready* take your own inner choice to turn your thoughts around and note what it is that you are "for" or what you *do* want or like or appreciate. It may take time and energy to get there, but the empowerment and relief you can feel are simply amazing!

Take the whole situation
and simply let it go—
just for today.

Week 10
Let Yourself Off the Hook

Have you ever noticed that almost everyone has areas in life that just seem easy? For some people relationships seem always to be loving and respectful; for others money has never been an issue; for some it has always been status quo to have a healthy, strong body; others have always had a fulfilling career or hobby; and some people have always had a deep sense of meaning and purpose in their lives. Cool. Along with having some areas that seem easier, we also each have parts of our life that seem much less easy—difficult even. Right now I want to talk about those areas.

I think we are really good at putting great effort—often in the form of self-criticism and stress—into our challenging situations whether they be worrisome finances, strained relationships, declining health, work challenges, or something different. So today, just for a few minutes, I want you to try something radical. I want you to let yourself off the hook. I am asking that you take whatever has been weighing on you, whatever has been worrying you, or taking a lot of your mental and emotional energy, whatever feels like it has been a chronic challenge—and I want you to put it down mentally, and stop working on it. Take the whole situation and simply let it go—just for today.

I know sometimes it sounds like I am promoting irresponsibility, but truly I am not. When you go over and over a challenging issue, especially if it has been around long enough to become a troubling habit or pattern, are you aware that you often use the same

Notice that you feel
some softening
and release.

mental, emotional, and physical efforts each time the situation comes up? And that those efforts have not yet worked to heal, change, or better the situation? That's not a criticism; it's just something I have noticed about myself and many others I have trained and coached.

In the spirit of trying something completely different, here is your provocation for this week. Bring your attention as fully and honestly as you can to something that has been causing you stress, fear, or worry. Only pick one. If you are like most people, you may be surprised that it will take some courage to do the next part of this simple, powerful process. In your mind's eye create a clear image, picture, or thought of yourself in the difficult situation; see and feel yourself and your typical responses to the situation. Now with sincerity say to yourself the Ho'oponopono verse, an ancient Hawaiian prayer of healing and forgiveness: "I'm sorry. Please forgive me. I love you. Thank you. I'm sorry. Please forgive me. I love you. Thank you. I'm sorry. Please forgive me. I love you. Thank you."

Don't worry too much when your mental, logical voice comes in and asks things like, "What do I have to be sorry for? If I'm the one talking, who am I talking to? Who am I asking to forgive me and why? I'm not the one who needs to be sorry," and on and on. Just say the verse over and over as many times as feels right for you. You may have emotions surface. You may notice that you feel some softening and release around the challenging area. There is no right or wrong here, simply do the process. Sometimes I get new insights or perspectives and they seem always to be in line with my more expanded heart's intelligence. Just give it a try and see what happens for you. Thank you.

It's beautiful to think about and honor people, relationships, and experiences that are gone.

Week 11

Before it's Gone

I think we're funny—or strange. We have made a habit, as a culture, to mourn things after they are gone even more than we ever celebrated them while here. Do you remember listening to "Long Distance Dedications" aired on the radio during the American Top 40 countdown? Listeners would write letters about touching situations and send them in to the radio station. I loved it every time the host, Casey Kasem, would read one. They were always inspiring and often made me cry, in the good heart-opening way, because they were about people caring and loving. But much of the time the only reason they wrote the letter, the only reason they felt their heart open up enough to talk about it, was because the relationship had ended or the friend was gone: they broke up; the friend moved away; someone died, etc. It was because of the *ending* that they more profoundly knew how much they had appreciated the person or thing.

There is certainly nothing wrong with that. It's beautiful to think about and honor people, relationships, and experiences that are gone, particularly the ones that helped to uplift and better our lives. But I also want to remember—*while still in my present moment*—all the beautiful things that are in my life right now. We shortchange ourselves if we don't do that. We miss out on noticing all the things that make our lives amazing right now. I am not pretending that there are not difficulties and hardships. I am just saying, and knowing, that along with those challenges, along with what is not working, there are so many things that really

Along with what is not working, there are so many things that really are magical, beautiful, and good right now in most all of our lives.

are magical, beautiful, and good right now in most all of our lives. And I know that life—my life, your life—is infinitely better if we simply take note of them *before* they are gone. So your provocation for the week is to do just that. Write a list of 10 things, as grand or mundane as you want, currently in your life that you would miss if gone. The more specific you are the more you can feel it!

Here is one of my lists:

1. The connection I have with Nikolas, my bright, wildly alive, fabulous son
2. The awesome powers of intention and choice which are ever available to help me co-create the life I experience
3. My healthy heart and awesome, strong legs that can walk and dance and skip
4. "Grandma Betty" who is not only my wonderful mom, but better yet my dear, dear friend
5. That I can so easily laugh and love
6. The power of love and the brilliance of the mind
7. Living daily in Southwest Florida which often feels like paradise
8. Getting paid to do work that I love
9. Chris and all my other wonderful humans who help make my life so awesome
10. That I can so often feel my connection with the Universal Essence/God, with my soul, with my inner guidance, and with beautiful people all over the planet

There are people and things
around us–right now–
who add love and light
to our days if we
but notice them.

After you write your list then take a few minutes to feel the fullness of being happy about them, grateful for them *right now*, while they are still here.

Life is good, and even in the midst of losses and difficulties that are very real, there are people and things around us—right now—who matter and who add love and light to our days if we but notice them.

Isn't it interesting that at some point most of us got the idea that criticizing ourselves was the right thing to do?

Week 12

What You Should Know About Self-Criticism

Your provocation this week is simple. Clearly not easy, but simple. Stop criticizing yourself *about anything* just for the week—and see how you feel. And watch what happens around you. Think of something you have criticized yourself for over the years. Really think one up. Is it your weight? Or the way you do money? Or how you procrastinate? Or how you talk to your spouse or kid(s)? Or what your house looks like? Or what you eat? Or how you never finished a certain project? Now think about it for a minute and notice if it's still there, if it's still a challenge. Is it? It seems that for almost all of us the answer is, "Yes." It kind of cracks me up actually, how clear the implication is: criticism is not working. It is not having the intended effect. It does not make us change the thought, attitude, or behavior about which we are unhappy or critical.

Isn't it interesting that at some point most of us got the idea that criticizing ourselves was the right thing to do? Maybe because we watched everyone around us do it. Or maybe because we got criticized so much that we just started believing it's what we should be doing too. Or maybe it just feels like the grown-up, responsible thing to do. Maybe we are afraid that things won't change if we don't criticize ourselves. Or maybe it's just easier to criticize us than it is to love and appreciate how cool we really are. I don't know all the reasons, but I have noticed over the years as I have worked with

Criticism keeps us
stuck to what
we are criticizing.

individuals and groups, and as I have watched my own inclinations, that there is a tendency for us to be… well, just mean to us sometimes and to criticize ourselves on a relatively consistent basis.

Now I am all for disciplined effort. I am for us taking personal responsibility and making positive changes. I am for us looking at ourselves and our behaviors honestly and asking, "Is this working? Does this serve my highest vision of myself?" That kind of healthy, expansive self-evaluation moves us toward empowered, intentional changes. When I say self-criticism does not work I'm not talking about those things. I am talking about the negative parental-type messages that some people seem to have been born with, and many of us got from parents, coaches, church leaders, teachers, or other "authorities." It's the critical voice that says, "No matter what you do, it's not quite right enough. No matter who you are or who you become it will never be good enough. No matter how you do things, you should have done it better." And on and on. This week stop listening, stop repeating, stop rehearsing, and stop believing those negative messages. They were never true anyway.

Criticism keeps us stuck to what we are criticizing. It does NOT make it go away. Self-acceptance and self-love of who we are *in this very moment before we are any different* is what creates the freedom and power to move on and change things we want to change. It really is that simple—not easy, but simple. Self-criticism keeps us stuck in and to the situations we want to change; self-approval feels way harder to do but is where the true power comes from to change the things we have wanted desperately to change.

This week your provocation is just that. Let go of all

Feel what happens
to you as you let
self-approval slowly and
gracefully replace
the self-criticism.

self-criticism. You can do it, and it's worth doing. It's a choice. Then feel what happens to you day by day as you let self-approval slowly and gracefully begin to replace the self-criticism. And by the way, I'm certain that when we have the slightest willingness to do that, divine assistance will rush in to help. It really is amazing.

I think we all came
with meaning and purpose
etched brilliantly into
our hearts.

Week 13

The Way You Intended to Live

I wonder how many of us are living the way we intended to live. It's a powerful question really: *Am I living the way I intended to live?* I'm not talking about how I thought I was going to live, or how I expected to live based on my beliefs by the time I was in high school or college. I mean way before that.

I think we all came with meaning and purpose etched brilliantly into our hearts. I do. I think it's still there for every one of us. But as we get older we go through all sorts of cultural education, social norms, and other "training" that can put us to sleep. We create so many habits and expectations that the deep sense of meaning and purpose—that abiding direction and guidance of our hearts and souls—can get covered up. That's probably the best, and simplest, definition of stress that we could use—living a life that feels devoid of our true meaning and purpose. It squishes the soul and is exhausting and sad. But I know beyond a shadow of a doubt that the radiance and love within our hearts, that essence that always wants our highest and best, the inner intelligence that is intricately connected to living with meaning and purpose, can never be extinguished. Ever. Even if we feel squished up and tired and all "wrong" inside.

It doesn't matter how old you are, or how long you have been living a life that parents (or friends, spouses,

Right before you
go to bed each night
ask yourself, "How did I
truly intend to live?"

coaches, teachers, clergy) wanted you to live, or how many mistakes you think you have made. At any time in this amazing life process, as long as you are still breathing, you can begin again. You can begin to do things differently, to see things differently, to react and respond differently, to work and play differently, to *be* differently. You can. You can begin at this very moment to live more in line with the way you intended to live. We all can.

Perhaps, though, we think we don't know what that means. Or we're too tired to do anything about it. *But if we are simply willing to ask the question then the answers, the energy, and the passion will start to show up.* I know that is true. It's a Universal law and it must be so. When we decide to live our highest and grandest purpose, when we are willing to live the way we intended to live, however mundane or magnificent it may seem to be, beautiful things start to happen. Guidance and support come from all sorts of places: from people we love, from our own insights and ideas, from things we hear in movies and songs, from authors and speakers, from friends and co-workers, even from strangers around us.

But it's your choice first. You need only be willing enough to ask and then listen. If you already know that you aren't living the way you intended to live it can be scary. But also really empowering and exciting! So that is your provocation for the week. Throughout your days as you are working or playing ask often, "Is this how I intended to live?" Then just be present for a few long, deep breaths with whatever emerges. And right before you go to bed each night ask yourself, *"How did I truly intend to live?"* Be open and simply let the answers begin to wash through you.

What a beautiful question!

Am I willing to be present
and compassionate with
my own challenges
and difficulties?

Week 14

Are They Safe on the Pathways of Your Mind?

Years ago I heard a Unity minister, Phillip Pearson, ask the question, "Are people safe on the pathways of your mind?" Wow. What an important question. Particularly because I believe that what we are thinking, and therefore what we are holding in our hearts, is at least as important as our words and actions. Actually, I think that our thoughts in some ways are more important because they eventually *lead to* our words and actions.

I have a sister who is sick a lot. She has been that way her whole life. How can I keep her safe on the pathways of my mind? By having compassion for her experiences of sickness *and also* by seeing her well, strong, and capable as consistently as she sees herself sick.

I have a friend who feels overwhelmed and scared about her life circumstances right now. The circumstances are very real. How can I keep her safe on the pathways of my mind? I could be soft and really listen to her feelings, *yet at the same time* I could know her strength and ability to make changes even more firmly than she fears she cannot.

A minister I know is sad and disappointed because of what is happening with the finances in his church. What can I best do for him? To keep him safe on the pathways of my mind I can be present and compassionate with his challenge, *and* hold thoughts and visions of greater prosperity and well-being for everyone concerned.

Keep people everywhere, yourself included, safe on the pathways of your mind.

Actively engaging both sides—*being present with compassion AND holding a higher vision of strength*—is a beautiful answer to, "How do I keep people safe on the pathways of my mind?" It's not always easy to do both. However, if I don't attempt both I will never live up to the vision of myself that I most want—me living as a beneficial and uplifting presence. This is why. If I only dive into the "realness" of their "bad" situation, then it becomes a negative swirling vortex taking everyone further down. It helps solidify the difficulty of the situation. I can feel when conversations are going in that direction because the loving softness of compassion turns instead into a heavy, sticky negativity. Do you ever have those conversations? On the other hand, if I am only holding strong thoughts and visions of more well-being, *without first being truly present with the pain someone is feeling,* then I often shut my heart down and seem cold and distant.

The same question is so very important for you to ask yourself also. Am I safe on the pathways of my mind? Am I willing to be present and compassionate with my own challenges and difficulties—without being judgmental or critical—*and at the same time* trust in my own goodness and strength to make changes?

This is your provocation: to keep people everywhere, yourself included, safe on the pathways of your mind this week. Be soft and compassionate *and* be powerful and strong. It is a tall order, but worthy of your attention. At least it is for me. Join me!

I still think it's amazing
that my life experiences
so clearly parallel the
energies of my thoughts,
beliefs, and self-talk.

Week 15

The Power of Inner Speech

I heard a speaker quote from a Reader's Digest article on Self-Talk. According to the speaker, psychologists wrote the article and reported, "The power of inner speech shapes your life more than any other single force." More than any other single force! If that's true, and personally I think it is, the implications are huge. It means that we have not only an enormous amount of personal responsibility, but also an enormous amount of personal power to shift our lives in any direction we want. That is the deliciousness of this kind of work.

I remember feeling really excited when I first learned about self-talk, affirmations (positive, present tense "I" statements), and the possibility to create my life the way I wanted it. I still think it's amazing that my life experiences so clearly parallel the energies of my thoughts, beliefs, and self-talk. If you want to know what your self-talk is like, just look at your health, finances, relationships, environment, personal/spiritual growth, work, and time. What you are experiencing in those areas matches the general trend of your self-talk about that subject. How cool is that? Or frustrating.

Whether we know it or not, and whether we choose to act on it or not, these three things are true: First, we are in charge of our own inner dialogue and self-talk. Second, as we change our self-talk to more closely match what we *want* instead of what currently *is,* our life will slowly start to resemble the more positive

It's not always easy
to change negative
self talk–but it is
well worth
the effort.

circumstances. Third, it's not always easy to change negative self-talk—but it is well worth the effort.

This week's provocation can get you started. Notice how you *feel* as often as you can this week. Simply check in and become aware of how you are doing. If you are feeling anything on the "good" end of the emotional continuum, great. Just bask in the moment. If you are feeling anything on the "yucky" end of the emotional continuum, then assume your self-talk *in that moment* is not serving you well.

When that is the case do the following: First, become aware of what the challenge or difficulty is. For me, it has often been lack of having enough time. It could just as easily be something dealing with health, money, relationships, work, or any other situation. Next, take your own self-talk and describe the *opposite* of the challenge in short, easy sentences. Here are some examples in several different areas:

I love having more than enough time; I love the feeling of getting all my projects done easily; it feels great to be organized and ordered; I feel empowered when I have plenty of money; it's wonderful to have relationships with loving, respectful people; I love when my body feels lean and strong and healthy; I love when my day moves in an easy flow; I feel good when I remember that people have beautiful hearts; I love feeling peaceful and connected; it's awesome to remember that my life matters; I love sleeping well and waking up rested.

The choices of positive self-talk alternatives are endless. This week simply find what is bothering you in any given moment and then shift your self-talk to describe the other end of it. Feel the relief and empowerment that happens when you take your own self-talk, just for a few moments, and focus on what you want, what you like, what you love, what you hope for. Awesome!

Take three long,
slow breaths any time
you feel yourself
"hurrying."

Week 16

Body Matters

I like this title because I'm going to talk about matters of the body, but also because it reminds me that my body *matters*. Sometimes I think we get so busy that we treat our bodies as though they get in our way. How dare they get tired, or need to eat, or move—when I have all this work I need to do! Maybe you have never done this, but sometimes I need to go get a drink of water or go to the restroom, yet instead of going I catch myself waiting until I am done with my next few things—whatever those may be—before I decide to go. Not today. Today I listen to my body's messages. Make it your phrase for the week. *Today I listen to my body's messages.*

Can you imagine if a child said to you, "I need to go to the bathroom," or "These shoes hurt my feet," or "I'm really tired," and then you saying, "Well, you'll just have to wait because I'm too busy right now," or "Leave those shoes on because they look good," or "You can't go to bed yet, there's too much to do." Wouldn't that be ridiculous? Not to mention just plain mean.

Start treating yourself and your body with as much love and respect as you would someone you really care about and hold precious. Because you *are* precious.

Here is your provocation for the week. Each day go at a pace that makes your body feel good; eat things that help you feel good; spend more minutes around people who make you feel good and less around people who don't; drink as much water as your body asks for; wear clothes that feel good; sleep as many hours as you need in order to feel rested and energized. Simply

I understand
that everything
will not get done,
but perhaps things
will work out anyway!

notice what your body would need in order to feel good and then give a sincere attempt to do it. Here are a few specifics that you can practice as you begin to act on the remembrance that your wonderful body matters.

1. Take three long, slow breaths any time you feel yourself "hurrying" and also every time you sit down—in your car, at a meeting, on the couch, at the dinner table, at your desk, anywhere. Feel the gentle softening that happens as you do.

2. Follow this short series:

   A. Stretch your neck side to side a few times.

   B. Reach your arms up for a big stretch, opening your mouth wide and faking a yawn while you do so (maybe a real one will come out).

   C. Wrap your arms around you in a big hug then drop your chin down to your chest and relax forward. This gives the spine a wonderful stretch.

   D. Last, while sitting in a chair twist gently around (first to one side then the other) looking back until you feel a good twist—not too much, not too little.

3. Be willing to hear when your body says, "I'm tired now," and decide—even if just for one day—to honor it and go to bed. Yes, I understand that everything will not get done, but perhaps things will work out anyway!

Do you notice how pushing harder can make you even more frustrated and impatient?

Week 17

Shift

This is important. And it takes some mental effort. When something is not going well the tendency is often for us to tighten up and push harder. Do you notice how pushing harder can make you even more frustrated and impatient? Which then makes the situation feel worse, and ends up narrowing your thinking, and also narrowing the possibilities of a solution? That is because we can't get free from what is not working when we are in the mental and emotional space of, "It's not working." Positive, light-hearted outcomes don't come from thinking, feeling, and expecting more of what feels yucky or wrong. In a way that is just common sense understanding, but I am asking that you take it out of simple understanding and instead put it into practice.

This is your provocation for the week. If you ever find yourself in the midst of feeling like something is not working, whether it is regarding family or relationships, a project at home or work, a financial situation, a health challenge, or something else—intentionally shift out of that feeling. *Then* go back to the situation. It takes mental discipline but here is one way to do it. First, you have to decide to let yourself and the challenging situation off the hook, just for a bit. That is easier said than done sometimes, but it is greatly worth it. You are greatly worth it. Next, take a big breath and *think about or do something that you enjoy*, even if only for a few minutes. Surprising and beautiful things can happen when you do!

You have to decide
to let yourself and
the challenging situation
off the hook.

Some years ago when my son, Nikolas, was younger he was building a jet from a Lego set that was for older children. It was a complicated, impressive structure and he worked on it for quite some time. I was surprised how focused he stayed on his project.

Eventually, the process started to go not so well. Things started falling apart—literally. His Lego pieces started falling off the jet. The more things that went wrong the more he wanted it fixed and completed in time to show his dad when he got home. So he tried to go faster. And more things fell apart. Within about 10 minutes he was really upset; he had pushed hard enough to get tired, frustrated, sad, and "mad at the Legos and the Universe!" he declared.

So I invited him outside with me to look at our two little turtles and all the tadpoles that had decided to come and live with us. Turtles and tadpoles rock! At first he didn't want to stop working and come with me, but I gently persisted. "Just for a few minutes," I said. He finally came outside with me and started looking at the two yellow-bellied sliders and the baby tadpoles we had on our back patio in a big tub. And I watched him shift. I watched all the brightness and ease come back into him, come back through him. It was beautiful. Then he went back in and finished his Lego jet. And it was beautiful too!

Even if you think you cannot really do it, or perhaps that it is irresponsible to try, this week when something is not going as well as you would like it to, make a sincere attempt to shift to a more positive inner experience first, and *then* continue to work on whatever needs your attention. I'll do the same.

Imagine that you
can breathe in and out
through the area
of your heart.

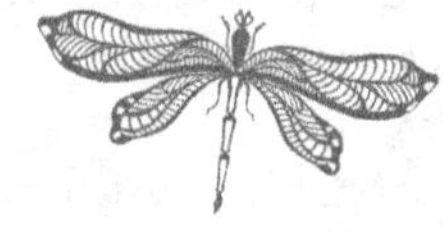

Week 18

Sleep Well

Do you ever have those nights when it takes a while to quiet your mind enough to fall asleep? Or those nights when you fall asleep but wake up a few hours later unable to go back to sleep? How about when you wake up in the morning and feel like you have been "going" all night long? I do. I read a disturbing statistic by the American Psychological Association (APA) that said 48% of Americans lie awake in bed because of stress. That is a lot of people!

I went to a wonderful HeartMath training in California some years ago which focused on transforming stress and increasing resiliency. It is really beautiful work. While I was there one of the trainers described something she does before she falls asleep every night. She said it always makes her "sleep like a baby." Nikolas, my son, woke up every hour and fifteen minutes—like clockwork—when he was a baby, so I don't really want that! But, of course, what she was talking about was having those wonderful nights where you sleep deeply and soundly. I love those nights—and the following mornings when I wake up rested and refreshed. I want way more of those awesome nights! I love waking up feeling energized and ready for the new day. So I decided to try the trainer's process while I was there. *I slept better in those few nights than I had in a very long time.* And since then, every time I remember to do it—or perhaps more honestly, whenever I decide to take the *effort* to do it—the same wonderful thing happens. I sleep wonderfully, and deeply, and wake up feeling beautifully alive and well.

Spend a full 10–20 minutes focusing on people, situations, or things that you love or appreciate.

So it is your provocation for the week. After you have gotten completely ready for bed, do the following steps. I do it sitting up so I don't fall asleep, but you decide what serves you best:

Become aware of your heart. You can think about it, feel it, visualize it, or sense it in any way you want to. You can focus on the physiological heart or the energetic heart. There is no right or wrong way. Next, begin to imagine that you can breathe in and out through the area of your heart—about 4-5 slow counts in, and 4-5 slow counts out. Do several rounds of this breathing. Now for the really good part spend a full 10-20 minutes focusing on people (pets count too!), situations, or things that you love or appreciate. Work toward *feeling* appreciation and love, and then *radiate those feelings through yourself first and then out to others.* You can radiate that feeling of love or appreciation to one special person or to a whole list.

Be patient and intend to sustain that warm, full, powerful feeling of love or caring for 10-20 minutes. Bask there until you drift off to sleep.

There is a quote that I love written by Unity Church's co-founder, Charles Fillmore. When he was 94 years old he wrote, "I fairly sizzle with zeal and enthusiasm and I spring forth to do the things that ought to be done by me." At 94! I bet he was sleeping well. Here's to all of us feeling full of energy, enthusiasm, and well-being each day when we wake up!

Self-love is what softens the impatience, doubt, and even hopelessness that can arise.

Week 19

The Truth about Discipline

If you think about positive changes that so many of us reach for—losing weight, healing relationships, increasing wealth, strengthening spiritual connection, starting an exercise program, finishing a creative project, etc.—they all take discipline to accomplish successfully. Without it they remain good ideas, but carry little hope of actually coming to fruition. And do you notice that we have issues with discipline?

Discipline is associated with what we have told ourselves we "should" be doing but probably aren't: eating the "right" kinds of foods, exercising more, quitting smoking, getting finances in order, even meditating more. When we don't do what we "should" do guilt can creep in. Not that I mean to be rebellious, but when I feel guilty about something it makes me *less* likely to do the "right" thing. Then there is the whole "being disciplined" thing associated with authorities. If we need to be "disciplined" it's probably because we aren't doing what "they" want us to do. It cracks me up, but it's true that when I feel as if someone is trying to *make* me do something, I get resentful and even more rebellious—which ironically keeps me from doing what probably would have served me well.

So the challenge is that we know lasting change can't happen without the commitment to discipline, but too often we seem to lack enough of it to follow through.

Consistency means to choose the new behavior, new action, new thought pattern, just because it will serve you well to choose it.

Maybe a new perspective, a new definition, would help. It has for me.

Here is my new definition of true discipline and it is your provocation this week to experiment with it. *Discipline is the art of bringing together consistency, self-love, and patience when you are working toward a specific goal or purpose.* How cool is that? Way less oppressive. Here *consistency* just means to choose to do something again and again—not because "they" say you should and not because you will be "wrong" if you don't. From a place of strong intention it means to choose the new behavior, new action, new thought pattern—even if it is difficult—just because it will serve you well to choose it. And then choose it again, and then again. Gently, firmly, and with no guilt. No drama or conflict or need to make anyone wrong—simply choose the desired attitude or action consistently.

The second component of true discipline is *self-love.* When you are attempting the exciting but difficult task of changing a habit or life circumstance, self-love is what softens the impatience, doubt, self-criticism, dissatisfaction, and even hopelessness that can arise. It is the infinitely magical attribute that calls you toward your grander possibilities, yet at the same time honors exactly where you are in each moment. Self-love uncovers the courage and strength needed for the consistency of discipline.

The third ingredient of this new discipline definition is *patience* and it is vitally important if you really want to make changes. Nothing adds grace and ease to the process of transformation as fully as patience does. It releases you from the suffocating pressure to hurry; it takes away the urgent need for things to be different this very minute. And paradoxically, it is only when you

Patience accesses a deep knowing that everything is already in perfect order even when it seems it is not.

quiet the constant drumming that says "I must hurry! This must change right away!" that things begin to change more quickly, gracefully, and effortlessly anyway. Once I heard the late Dr. Wayne Dyer say, "Infinite patience produces immediate results." Brilliant. Feel the beautiful truth in that. Patience accesses a deep knowing that everything is already in perfect order even when it seems it is not, and even when your good seems yet out of reach.

This week play in the relief and power that comes about by changing your definition of discipline and then begin to put the three components—consistency, self-love, and patience—into motion with your desired changes. May you be wonderfully surprised and pleased with yourself and your results!

Today I will work
toward my happiness
and well-being.

Week 20

Were You Happy?

I was thinking about something that opened my heart and gave me a higher perspective. Now it's your provocation for the week. Imagine you are 86 years old and a bright-eyed, happy little kid is asking you all sorts of wonderful questions. Imagine him or her being really interested in you and your life, and wanting to know all about what you have done, who you have been, challenges you have had, and how you dealt with them. Imagine his or her eyes filled with curiosity and a depth of being that helps you feel alive as you talk. Imagine being asked about your childhood, teen years, young adult years, and later adult life by someone who really wants to hear all of your (rebellious, funny, sad, real) stories.

You get to go through and talk about all of your accomplishments and regrets; all of the people you loved and the ones who got away; the experiences that made you laugh and the ones that hurt a lot; all of the things that ever weighed on you as if there was no solution and how you made it through them anyway; times when you felt guilty or ashamed, and times when you were proud of yourself; and on and on. What if that person was so present that you could *feel yourself* again as you answered all the questions?

And then imagine him or her looking right into your eyes and asking, "And were you happy?"

There is a good chance that most of you reading this are not yet 86 years old. Don't wait until then to look back and ask, "Have I been happy?"

You are allowed
to feel happy
and alive.

With all of the chaos and stress that so many are feeling right now at work, at home, financially, with health, or in relationships, take a minute to step back and ask a really simple, really hard question: Am I happy? If you are happy much of the time, then keep doing more of what you are doing and celebrate all the good you are experiencing. If you honestly say, "No," then perhaps it is time for a change—a change of habits, a change of priorities, a change of heart.

You are allowed to feel happy and alive. You are allowed to breathe easily and enjoy your life—even in the midst of chaos. You are. We all are. It is not Pollyanna or fluffy. It's not even irresponsible or selfish. It is uplifting and empowering for all of us when even *one of us* says, "Today I will work toward my happiness and well-being—because it matters. Because I matter."

Someone asked me, "Are *you* happy?" and I was silent for a moment really thinking about it. And then I answered honestly, "There are always things I want to change, expand, and get better. But yes—many, many moments of my life I am simply happy." I think that is because I have decided it is worth working toward. And that I am worth it.

Today, no matter where you are, decide that you are worth it. Because as simply and profoundly as I can say it—you are.

The next time you find
yourself in that funky,
yucky, squished up,
pressed on place
just let yourself
be there—fully.

Week 21

Celebrate the Funk!

This is for the next time you find yourself feeling "off" in some way… out of sorts, in a funk, or just generally yucky. I had a relieving insight. I'm really big on personal responsibility and our own ability to create lives we love, lives lived with lots of peaceful, happy, fulfilling moments. Do you ever find that knowing you are responsible for the life you create is sometimes empowering and wonderful, but sometimes just plain hard?

"Take your own discipline to think about things you are appreciative of; spend some time each day to breathe consciously and be present in the moment; move patiently but consistently toward goals that make your heart sing; imagine yourself already living the way you want to live; practice your relationships the way you would like them to be; love your warts as much as your beautiful parts; do what you need to do in order to nurture yourself," and on and on.

Most of the time I love remembering those things and working toward them. And truly, it serves us so well to take our energy to participate in those practices. Every once in a while, though—not that you need it, but here is permission just because it is nice to have—just allow yourself to wallow in the funk. That was my big insight: that I could just be there feeling weird and "off" and funky, and *not* try so hard in that moment to get somewhere different. Of course I like it better when I feel easy, happy, light, and intentional. And of course I will always continue to do this work. But

Life is beautiful that way.

maybe part of doing this conscious work of creating lives we love, lives with less stress and more well-being, is to just allow ourselves moments when things feel "not right" somehow. And not push on ourselves too hard about it, and simply trust that soon enough, "This too shall pass."

I watch my cool son who is normally bright and happy without much effort. Every once in a while he just feels "out of sorts." He gets in a funk. When it happens I usually know enough, trust enough, love enough, to give him the space to just *be*, to let him feel the way he is feeling without pushing on him emotionally or energetically to "snap out of it." I already know somehow that soon enough he will come out the other side.

So what if we did that with ourselves too? What if we decided to have that much trust and ease with ourselves also?

Here is your provocation. The next time you find yourself in that funky, yucky, squished up, pressed on place *just let yourself be there—fully*. Whether you are there for seemingly no reason at all or for lots and lots of good reasons, just let yourself off the hook. For as long as it feels right to do it, let yourself feel and be however you are. Be gentle and loving and supportive with you the same way you would want to be for a cool, precious, beautiful, amazing kid. Because while we may not be that young in terms of the number of years we have lived, in so many ways we *are* cool, precious, beautiful, amazing kids.

So relax and even celebrate your funk the next time it happens. Interestingly, when you do that it helps it pass much more quickly and gracefully anyway. Life is beautiful that way, and I am truly grateful for that.

What is right is to be gentle, loving, and kind with ourselves.

Week 22

Right or Easy?

I love Harry Potter. I was re-watching the DVDs and in one of them Dumbledore, the wise, empowered, "good" wizard says that it is time, "To do what is right, not what is easy." I started thinking about how true that is if we all want to create beautiful lives we love. I can feel it in my gut sometimes. When you hear the word "right" it's easy to think of it in terms of "right vs. wrong," "morally right," or "right" based on what you think you "should" do. That's not what I am talking about. When I think of doing "what's right" it means what is right from the guidance of my own inner knowing, from my heart's alignment, from the depth of my soul. It is that which feels powerful, positive, light, and loving.

I don't think doing what is right always has to be different from what is easy. I love when they are the same choice, but sometimes they simply are not. For instance: staying up late to watch TV or doing more busy work, versus going to bed early enough to feel rested, happy, and excited about the new day. What is usually *right* for me is to go to bed earlier and feel more present, happy, and alive the next day; what is *easy* is to stay up later and just keep going. Another choice I find challenging: taking a good chunk of my weekend to clean the house and do other chores, versus going outside and doing something fun. Here is where it gets interesting. Sometimes what is *right* for me is to have my house look and feel beautiful by doing the cleaning, but sometimes it is to blow it all off and play with my family or friends. There is no

Treat yourself like the magnificent, wondrous, courageous, strong being you are.

blanket answer or situation that is always *right*, because it depends on what sits full, present, right, and real within each of us in that specific moment.

Your provocation this week is to be present enough and courageous enough to ask daily—even with mundane, seemingly insignificant choices, "If I were going to choose *what is right*, instead of just *what is easy*, what would I choose?" Would I focus on someone else's behavior or decide to focus on my own attitudes and actions? Start on a creative project or answer more e-mails? Stay late at work or go home on time? Work out or take the day off? Stay busy or take some time to meditate or simply breathe?

And this is *not* about feeling guilty. Feeling bad, guilty, or critical of ourselves when we think we have not made our very best choice can feel like the *easiest* thing to do out of habit. But I feel certain that what is *right* is to be gentle, loving, and kind with ourselves even when we do not always choose what serves us well.

There are so many times when the choices seem so little that they probably don't really matter. *But it is all of those little choices added up together that either lead us to living our highest and best, making a positive difference, and helping to heal and uplift—or not.* And I think we don't give ourselves enough credit. The truth is you are good. You are worthy. And you are capable of doing beautiful, important things. So this week treat yourself like the magnificent, wondrous, courageous, strong being you are and ask yourself choice by choice, "If I choose what is *right* instead of just what is *easy*, what will I do right now?" And then watch how you make a bigger difference than you ever thought possible!

Real stress relief,
happiness, and well being
are created from
teeny, tiny decisions
made moment
by moment.

Week 23

For You Today

I have one of those footbath massager things in my closet. I looked at it the other day and realized that though I love how it feels, I haven't used it in a while. I also have a small, beautiful book by Jon Kabat-Zinn that was a gift to me. It's called *Letting Everything Become Your Teacher: 100 Lessons in Mindfulness.* Though I love his work and have the book on my nightstand to help me remember to take moments to be truly present in my life, I had not flipped through it in several nights. As I was noticing those things this crystal clear thought came through me: *Rarely is it my lack of abilities, information, resources, or even time that keeps me from experiencing well-being in this moment; it's simply my lack of deciding—right now—to be* FOR *me enough to do anything about it.* I was surprised by the simplicity and importance of the awareness. And in that moment, probably because of the power within that straightforward awareness, I felt freer and lighter.

Sometimes, even though I play in this self-care "stuff" a lot, I get caught up in the belief, or maybe the habit, that I need to wait until a specific time or different day to "do" stress relief, personal empowerment, or self-care. After all, it's easy to do self-care when I am visualizing, meditating, having a massage, taking a vacation day, laughing with friends, or feeling the wind at the beach.

But what about right this minute? If I don't want to take the time to run warm water and stick my feet in the footbath for a few minutes tonight, can I at least squeeze my toes around a few times right now? Or feel my breath

You are good,
and beautiful,
and you are allowed
to feel happy
and well!

coming in and out slowly? Can I look at the pictures on my bulletin board from my son and appreciate how cool they are? Or do a few shoulder rolls? Can I dwell on what really matters to me? Can I invite my shoulders to soften and feel my back against the chair for a moment? Can I think about someone I love and surround him or her with light, love, appreciation, and well-being? Can I remember, just for a moment, that I want to make a positive difference while I am here on the planet?

Real stress relief, happiness, and well-being are created from teeny, tiny decisions made moment by moment. Thus, your provocation for the week is simply this. Be FOR you today with the smallest of choices. Every moment you remember this provocation, simply ask yourself, "What is one small choice I can make in this moment that serves me well?" No choice is too small. They all matter. And if you have trouble coming up with something try just noticing your breath for a few seconds, or remembering a time when you felt particularly happy. That's it. And by the way, each time I roll my shoulders or take a slow intentional breath it feels great—which is a good enough reason to do something!

You are good, and beautiful, and you are allowed to feel happy and well!

Your fullness and happiness matter!

Week 24

Feeling Frisky

When people talk about "stress reduction" what usually comes up first are things like breathing, meditation, yoga, relaxation, or massage. I love those things! They bring me a wonderful sense of peacefulness and nurturing as they move me away from the high-stress, fast-paced, incessant "busyness" of continually having too much to do. There is another part of true stress reduction and self-care, however, which I want to focus on in this week's provocation. Do you ever have times when it feels like the real problem isn't just all the hurrying and rushing, but that it may also be the squishing, deadening, or sleepiness you feel from having lived for days, weeks, months, or longer without feeling truly awake, inspired, frisky, or alive? Without these—without the powerful childlike qualities of feeling excited about life, being playful and imaginative, feeling drawn to accomplish great things, and being passionate about new adventures—stress reduction processes will only be a shadow of what they could be.

In light of that awareness here are some important questions to inspire your friskiness. Who or what makes you really laugh? What have you ever done, or do now, that makes you feel inspired? No matter your age, what is one "great" thing you could accomplish—however you define it? What can you spend hours of effort doing that feels more like play than work? What sorts of conversations and topics make you feel alive and engaged? If limited time, money, health, or energy

What could you do
that makes you feel
playful, creative,
passionate, curious,
and fully awake?

were not issues, what could you do that makes you feel playful, creative, passionate, curious, and fully awake? Who or what makes your heart sing?

Your provocation for the week is simple… and wonderful! Go through the list of questions above and answer each of them. You can think through your answers, say them aloud, or write them down. As you do this notice how you feel, both as you read each question and as your answers start to emerge. Bask in the deliciousness of starting to remember what makes you feel really alive. Then, take one step—no matter how small or large—toward an action which is in alignment with an answer to one of those questions.

Your fullness and happiness matter!

I think most of us
have been going about it
backwards as we wait to
be happy until we accomplish
more things on our lists.

Week 25

Now Instead of Then

Here is a cool insight that has to do with our never-ending lists, our goal-setting, and our urge to create the things we want to have or do: even when we accomplish something else, *how we have been treating ourselves is probably how we are going to continue treating ourselves—unless we consciously decide otherwise.* If I am unhappy with and critical of myself today, there is a good chance that I am going to treat myself like that even when I lose my 10, 20, even 30 pounds. If I always treat myself as if I am rushed and in a hurry, there is a good chance that even when I have grown, changed, or ended my career that I am still going to be in the habit of feeling rushed and in a hurry. If I always worry about not having enough money, there is a good chance that I will still be worried about it even as I begin to make more and more money.

What shall we do with this? I am not saying that it is not a beautiful, healthy, empowered thing to want to make changes and move forward toward our goals and plans. On the contrary—I think it is one of the most important and beneficial things we can do! But I think most of us have been going about it backwards as we wait to be happy until we accomplish more things on our lists. If you keep *doing* things first (trying to lose weight, make more money, expand or change careers, get into or out of a relationship, etc.) in hopes that you will eventually *feel* and *be* happier, and if you look over your life and notice that it has not worked yet, then this week try it a different way.

Start treating your body now with the love and respect you think you will feel for it once it is finally healthy.

Start treating your body *now* with the love and respect you think you will feel for it once it is finally healthy, strong, skinny, young, or whatever other word you like. Start walking, driving, breathing, and acting as if you have all the time in the world *now* even while your To-Do List is yet unfinished. Start giving to others, planning vacations, learning about investing, saving a portion of your income, or organizing your bills *now* even before the extra income has shown up.

Your provocation this week is simply this. Ask yourself, "How will I act, how will I treat myself, how will I treat others, how will I talk and breathe and move—when my goal is reached?" And then, just for this week, start doing that. The crazy thing is, when you start doing that first, the changes you have been wanting begin to show up in much more graceful ways.

I love this stuff.

That awareness creates
my point of power to
choose differently
when I want to.

Week 26

How Foods Feel

I like food. There are so many foods we are supposed to stay away from, or at least limit, according to experts in the industry. Depending on which dietician, nutritionist, physician, book, or PBS special you are currently in alignment with, here are some of the possible things to steer clear from: fats, red meat, all meat, carbs, anything not organic, anything not locally grown, all processed foods, MSG, hydrogenated oils, dairy, salty snacks, sugary snacks, alcohol, corn syrup, any grain that is not a whole grain, white anything (flour, rice, bread, sugar, pasta), preservatives, and on and on.

It can be a bit much. So I have an idea. While there is a good possibility that many of the different eating guidelines have merit, before you pick which foods to embrace and which to throw away, do something really awesome. Instead of basing your decision on logical arguments from all the external authorities, decide first *how foods feel—to you.* This is your provocation and it is really wonderful. This week intend to be fully present and mindful of you and your food before, during, and after you eat. How does your food look? Does your whole body want it or simply your taste buds? How does it smell? Is your body asking for something different instead? Can you really taste the food or are you rushing through it? Then, and this is the important part—*10 to 20 minutes after you have eaten, notice how you feel physically, mentally, and emotionally.* Are you sluggish or energized? Do you have any aches? Are you mentally clear or foggy? Do you feel "deadened" and numb, or frisky and alive?

You deserve to
feel good.

Don't make it a judgmental, criticism thing; just notice how you are doing. You may uncover something that can be really helpful.

Here is what I have found. Generally, food serves me well, unless I am using it for stress-reduction or relief, then not so much. Sometimes I eat sugary food because I consciously choose to have a bit of the yummy taste. Other times I crave it and it feels not so much a conscious choice, but rather like I "need" it. Most often those times are: when I feel sleepy or drained during an afternoon lull; when I feel nervous, anxious, mad, or even excited about something; when I am tired from not getting enough quality sleep; when I am low on water but don't realize I am thirsty. When I eat something sweet at those times, it tastes good on my tongue as I eat it. It also feels like it brings me some sort of relief. Then, shortly afterward I usually feel more tired, drained, sluggish, and sometimes even mean. No fun really, but it is actually cool to know—because that awareness creates my point of power to be able to choose differently if and when I want to.

Our bodies rock! Your body rocks! Notice it this week. You have the opportunity to live in it fully, to listen to it, and to take lavish, loving care of it. Not because you "should." Not because you need to "guilt yourself" into it. But quite simply, because you deserve to feel good. Whether or not anyone ever told you that, it is true. *You deserve to feel good.* And noticing how foods feel from inside you is an amazing and powerful way to put that knowing into practice.

Don't forget that
things can be different
even if they've been
the same way
for a long time.

Week 27

Don't Forget

I love to feel happy. I love to feel peaceful, strong, confident, and loving. I love to be on purpose and feel connected to the still small voice of love within me. I love to feel a balance between challenge, effort, and empowerment on one hand; and respite, ease, and basking on the other. I love to play in all of my work, and I also love having the free time to enjoy myself, my loved ones, and my life outside of work. Some days I experience those things so fully that my heart feels as if it's going to burst open with gratitude. Other days I don't—at all.

I was working with a cool high school kid and his mom because they both said they needed help with stress reduction. When I asked, "What do you most want?" the son answered, "Just to feel happy," and the mom, "To feel more peace." Yes. So many of us are going day to day without experiencing some of the simplest and most profound desires of our hearts like feeling loved, happy, peaceful, passionate, content, fulfilled, alive, or that life has meaning. But even worse is the growing numbers of people who seem to have fallen asleep to the possibility that *it can be different.* "It's just the way it is," seems to have become our mantra. As simplistic as this sounds, please hear the importance of it: it is true that things *are* the way they *are*—but only until they aren't anymore. And you have the power to make changes. But that only usually happens small choice by small choice. And you first have to remember, at some level of your being, that changes are even possible.

You can create
a life you love.

So this is your provocation for the week. Don't forget that you are allowed to be happy and less stressed—even if that doesn't seem possible right now. Don't forget that Life is good and is always *for* you—even if that doesn't seem true right now. Don't forget that things can be different—even if they've been the same way for a long time. Don't forget the utter possibility that you can create a life you love. Because I promise you no matter how ridiculous it sounds, that possibility is very real.

And don't forget that when you want something so very much—like a healthier body, easier finances, better relationships, work that makes your heart sing, or simply more time to breathe and enjoy your life—*it means that not only is it a possibility, but also your responsibility to create it.* Because you can. And because we are here to make a positive difference on the planet—every one of us—even if we forgot that. If it is a stretch for you to remember that for yourself, then do it for everyone else. Because even one radiantly alive, loving, compassionate, wildly expanded, happy human being can make a huge positive difference for the rest of us. Decide this week to be that one!

Whatever you find yourself
working on this week,
ask yourself,
"How will I
feel when it is
successfully
completed?"

Week 28

Feelings First, Then Actions

I know it sounds too simplistic, but I believe we often do the things we do because we think we'll feel better having done them. Look at whatever is often on your plate. Has it become a habit to think you are doing them just because they "need" to get done? This week go one step further and become aware of how you think you will *feel* when some of your things get done.

Here are some of my own examples:

I respond to work e-mails because… I feel responsible, happy, and relieved when I'm done; I clean the house and do laundry because… I feel good when things are clean and ready for our family to use; I work on my speaking and writing career because… I feel alive, frisky, happy, and "right" internally when I do; I work on my never-ending To-Do List because… I feel wonderfully satisfied, capable, and relieved when I get finished with some of the things on the list; I work on eating less sugar because… I feel energized, lighter, more focused, and happy with myself when I do; I meditate, pray, and focus on my connection with God/Source because… I feel peaceful, loving, inspired, empowered, radiant, and spiritually connected when I do; I pay bills because… I feel happy and grateful for having access to, living in, and using all of the things that we pay for; I work out and dance because… I feel healthy, alive, joyful, strong, rhythmic, and beautiful when I do; I spend time playing with, and taking care

The magic is that
when we create
the feelings first, then
the actions become
way easier.

of, friends and family because… I feel loving, loved, funny, childlike, playful, compassionate, silly, happy, relaxed, and appreciative when I do.

There is a good chance that the list of what you "need" to do is endless. And that some of those things are not any fun to do. There is also a good chance that sometimes it feels like you don't have enough time, energy, or money to do them all. So here is your provocation, because it can really make a positive difference if you do it. Whatever you find yourself working on this week, ask yourself, "How will I feel when it is successfully completed?" Then take a few moments to *practice that feeling first*—satisfied, happy, peaceful, empowered, content, creative, loving, passionate—*before you begin to do the actions needed to get it done.* Feelings first, then actions.

Sometimes my project at home is going through the mail/filing/paper pile that has stacked up over a couple of weeks–yuck! What does it feel like to me when it's done? Order, relief, lightness, and me being proud of myself. Ahhh!

It may not be easy to conjure order, relief, lightness, and being proud of me *before* the "thing" is accomplished, but *it is possible.* And the magic is that when we create the feelings *first,* then the actions become way easier, more direct, and even more fun to take.

Here's to all of us getting our "things" done with more grace by thoroughly enjoying the feelings of completion and accomplishment *before* we take the needed actions. Try it and watch what happens!

There is something amazing about appreciation.

Week 29

Wave of Appreciation

There is something amazing about appreciation. It's like a wonder drug that powerfully assists the person using it, but positively affects everyone else too. Did you know that at anytime, anyplace, you can shift your thoughts and move toward appreciation? And that when you do a cascade of beautiful things can happen?

Here are some of the things that happen for me when I practice intentional appreciation: I notice that anything that was worrying me, or preoccupying me, simply softens into the background (and sometimes even goes away); I feel my muscles relax and soften in my shoulders which is where I often hold tension; I feel mentally more clear, focused, and creative after I practice appreciation; if I want a healthier, higher, more loving or effective perspective on something that has been challenging me, I get one; if I am feeling too fast or busy it calms me down and centers me; if I am feeling fatigued or bored it energizes and inspires me; and most importantly, I feel emotionally wonderful—grateful, easy, light, happy, at peace, and deliciously full. All of those things just from intentionally choosing to practice appreciation. Very cool.

Since it works so beautifully for me I thought it would be a great provocation for you too! So here it is. Though you can practice appreciating any way you want to, here is a wonderful—and powerful—practice to try. I call it the Wave of Appreciation. Imagine that a great wave of love, light, caring, compassion, or appreciation is going to build up and then rush through, the same

Imagine feeling
an increased sense
of relief, peace, love,
strength, and well-being.

way an ocean wave does. The appreciation or love of this powerful wave can come from your own heart or soul, from God/Source, from a beautiful stream of light, or any other way that feels right when you think about or visualize it. There are four parts to this wave's activity:

First, imagine it moving through *you*—touching and blessing every cell of your wonderful body, every thought you think, every habit you have, every belief, every word, every attitude, every action you take, and everything you have ever experienced—the good and the not-so-good.

Second, feel or see the Wave of Appreciation moving out past you and blessing *all* of the important and mundane "stuff" around you—your bed, the shower, food, lights, appliances, toothpaste, shampoo, toilets, counters, vehicles, bank accounts, buildings, clothing, dishes, your desk and computer, cell phones, social media, televisions and other electronic screens, books, files, mail (even the bills), furniture, your garage, your lawnmower, and on and on. Imagine the Wave continuing out and rushing over all of nature: plants, grass, rocks, trees, wind, water, birds, clouds, and animals everywhere. See them filled up with this Wave and intend to feel appreciation for all of these things.

Third, imagine this wave getting stronger and more powerful. Now intentionally direct it toward and through all the people and things you hold most dear to your heart. Imagine them feeling this Wave of Appreciation and being blessed by it. Imagine them all feeling an increased sense of relief, peace, love, strength, and well-being.

Finally, allow the Wave of Appreciation to expand out to everyone and everything all over the whole planet,

I don't think we know
how powerful we are to
affect positive change
for ourselves and
for others.
We are though.

and then to the planet itself. Like a great tsunami of compassion, caring, and appreciation moving through, blessing and loving everyone, everything, everywhere.

Then bask in how you feel. Sometimes I don't think we know how powerful we are to affect positive change for ourselves and for others. We are though.

I love playing
with inner guidance.

Week 30

Subtle Messages

I love playing with inner guidance. Whether you think of it as inner messages, higher knowing, heart's intelligence, the still small voice of God, your own higher self, internal guidance, intuition, or simply quiet awareness, it is a consistent—though subtle—inside "nudging" that is always with us, whether we notice it or not. The label doesn't really matter. Once I heard Dr. Deepak Chopra say intuition was "simply a heightened state of awareness." Whatever you want to call it, I find that my life is much more rich, fulfilling, and fun when I attempt to notice and follow it.

I remember a specific weekend some years ago when I followed it… and when I didn't. Maybe you can relate. I used to love it when I would hear Jeff, my ex-husband, playing in the pool and being silly with Nikolas, our son. One Memorial Day weekend when I heard them out there I got that little feeling to go join them. My head was not in the mood to follow through on the subtle inner message because I was already "doing something" inside. But I had been practicing following my inner guidance so I chose to stop my "busyness" and go in the pool with them instead. It was awesome! I felt overwhelmed with love and appreciation—for my family, my health, my consciousness, the Universal Essence, the mystery and the beauty of Life itself, my home, the swimming pool, living in Florida, the great big tree in the back, the dragonflies flying around everywhere (which I'm sure are magic!), having a weekend off to do whatever I wanted, and mostly just for *being*... It was really beautiful.

When we listen to those internal cues, no matter how mundane they seem, life is much more graceful, more peaceful, and more fulfilling in a million different ways.

It would be more fun to say, "End of story because I always follow my guidance." Except that isn't true.

Jeff had been wanting a new riding mower. That same Memorial Day weekend, before we left for our cookout, he got the "inclination" (yet another label for it) to look online for mowers. He found a really good one for a great price very close to where we were going to be. Cool. Jeff e-mailed to say he was very interested; then we left for our cookout. The guy called. I knew—from that subtle inner guidance feeling—that we should go right then; Jeff told me later that he also had the feeling that we should go right then. But we weren't in the mood to stop doing whatever we were doing, so we waited an hour. Just an hour. At the exact moment that we pulled into the guy's driveway we watched as two young gentlemen handed money to the seller for their newly purchased riding mower. Bummer.

Neither of these situations were life and death—they usually aren't. It's simply that when we listen to those internal cues, no matter how mundane they seem, life is much more graceful, more peaceful, and more fulfilling in a million different ways. And I have noticed that when I make a habit of following the *little* inner messages, it is then much easier to "hear" them when more serious or important situations arise.

Your provocation this week is to take note of your subtle messages and follow them—as unimportant or even impractical as they may seem. Use it as an experiment and see what happens!

Do you ever have things that you know you will feel great about doing once you do them, but instead of doing them you let other daily stuff get in the way?

Week 31

What I Need to Do

I just re-learned something really, really important. When I go through my days, as wonderful as they can often be, if I am putting off doing something that is meaningful and important to me, something that I know I need to do—I am a shell of what I could be. I know that sounds a little dramatic, but it's true. I can tell when I am putting off something that I "need" to do because while I still look and sound nice enough and still get things done, there is more of an edge to me. People that know me can sense that I am shorter and more impatient with people I care about.

I had been putting off writing. Which is strange because I feel awesome when I am writing, even just little bits at a time. Do you ever do that? Do you ever have things that you *know* you will feel great about doing once you do them, but instead of doing them you let other daily stuff get in the way? I noticed that I had been waiting until I had the time to do it in order to do much writing. But the days kept going by, and I stayed wonderfully busy with other things—and the "time to do it" kept not happening.

Then I started writing again anyway, even without the magic "extra" time. I don't even know why really. I just did. It's unbelievable how much more alive and full I feel when I simply do what I know is to be done by me, what I "need" to do—not based on some outside authority, but based on that inner knowing, based on what feels right and clear and good. I feel more focused and "on purpose" inside—and more joyful. I have had

Decide today
that you are worth
taking good care of.

other times when it was as simple as calling someone I care about, going through my pile of "stuff," going dancing, getting my finances more organized, or cleaning out a particular drawer. Whatever it is, we each have an inner guidance system that simply feels "off" if we are not doing something we *know* is to be done by us, something that would serve us well if we did it.

What is something that keeps pushing at you? What is something you know is important but you keep putting off? Your provocation this week is to answer those questions and then take just ten minutes to begin it. *Even if you know it will take much longer than that to complete, something almost magical seems to happen when you just start.* It is like a big procrastination layer comes off and you have more energy to move forward. Try it this week and see what happens—even if you only accomplish baby steps on it. If you do more, great. If you don't, great. Ten minutes. That's all it needs to be.

There is a quote by Thomas Edison that says, "If we did all the things we were capable of doing, we would literally astound ourselves." I want to astound myself! I want us all to.

Decide today that you are worth taking good care of. Then get started with something you "need" to do based upon a sincere intention to be aware of, and play in, your highest possibilities.

Autopilot mode
sucks the life out of us.
I start going on autopilot
when I feel tired
and overdone.

Week 32

Rescuing Yourself from Autopilot

I love when I take vacation days. I stop a lot of my "busyness" and I trade it for extra naps, walking, writing, dancing, and meditating. Awesome! I remember when I took some "stay-cation" days and a cool thing happened: I felt like I found myself again. Interesting, since I hadn't realized I was missing. Does that ever happen to you? Do you ever feel like you are going day by day making it through all the routines of work or home on autopilot, and all of a sudden you notice you are hardly even there? I think it happens even more if we don't enjoy our usual routines. I like many of mine. I love the people I get to be home with, and I love the people I get to work with. I enjoy what I do for work, and I enjoy what I do for play. But even though I truly get pleasure from many of the routines of my daily life, doing those things on autopilot is so much different from doing them consciously, by choice. Autopilot mode sucks the life out of us.

I start going on autopilot when I feel tired and overdone. It's my protective mode when I feel fried. And I feel more fried, tired, and overdone when I rush around on autopilot. It's one of those nasty downward spirals that adds to stress. While it's true that a week off from work can help get me back, I don't have to wait for vacations to remember to be present, and therefore to be more fulfilled and happy—both at home and at work. Neither do you! So here is a provocation to help bring

I don't have to wait for vacations to remember to be present, and therefore to be more fulfilled and happy.

relief and fullness back to your days when you may need it. Throughout the week ask yourself *why you are doing whatever you are doing.* If the first answer is "To get done," or "Because I have to," then ask again and again until you feel your heart move back into the answer.

Here is an example when I was writing one of my weekly "Blurbs."

"Why am I doing this?"

"Because I write these on Tuesdays."

"Why do I do that?"

"Because that's the day I send it out to people."

"Why are you doing that?"

"Because it is my highest intention and great hope that it will uplift or benefit someone in some way. And because I always feel happy and proud of myself when I complete one."

Ah, yes—*that* is why. You can do the same thing with anything you are working on, whether personal or professional, simply by asking until once again you feel the *real* reason, the primary reason, the heartfelt reason why you are doing it all anyway.

"Why do I do these things that sometimes feel like 'too much'?"

"Because I love being the best mom I can be."

"Because I feel great when my house is clean and beautiful."

"Because I am happy when there are wonderful groceries and healthy dinners to eat."

"Because I really like doing my job well."

"Because it feels awesome to have a strong body."

"Because I love to feel my spiritual connection."

"Because it rocks to get paid for doing my work."

"Because I feel proud of helping provide for my family."

Bring your heart
back into why
you actually do
what you do.

"Because I love helping people."

The list can go on and on. When you bring your heart back into *why* you actually do what you do—then simplicity, relief, fullness, love, and well-being move into and through your day-to-day routines. That for me is worth the effort!

I want us all to try less.
And live more.
And breathe more.

Week 33

The Art of Trying Less

I think we try too much. Too hard, too often, too much. We even *try* to relax. The word "trying" conjures up a certain picture for me which feels very different from qualities I love including things like *ease, strength, simplicity, clarity, power,* and *focus.* Do you ever notice that sometimes "trying" can feel like heavy, endless effort... because if you are still *trying* to do something then you obviously haven't succeeded?

I want us all to try less. And live more. And breathe more. I think kids and animals do this really well. Instead of "trying," they are either *doing* something—with commitment, passion, intensity, and often humor, or they are *not doing*—such as basking in a sunny afternoon nap, or sleeping peacefully through the night. Either way, they are doing what they are doing—fully.

When I say I want us to try less it can sound like I am promoting non-productive, lazy, or irresponsible behaviors. The opposite is true really. One of my favorite things is knowing with certainty that every one of us, no matter our age or experience, is continually being called to live a life of great purpose, and that when we do we make beautiful, positive changes for our world. For that to happen we have to have our physical, emotional, and spiritual "tanks" full. We need to feel a sense of buoyancy and resiliency; we need to have our inner convictions primed and ready for action *and* non-action.

But when we are always "trying" so hard, with almost everything in our life, it can squish us up until we feel exhausted on every level. When that happens we don't

Every one of us is
continually being called
to live a life
of great purpose.

have access to what we really need for action: passion, strength, and intensity; nor do we have access to what allows for true non-action: peace, stillness, clarity. And of course, it is both sides that we need in order to live radiantly, truly as our highest and best. We need the power and strength of fully doing *and* the relaxation and ease of fully not doing. "Trying" puts us right in the middle where we don't have access to either side: the effort needed for meaningful action or the enjoyment of surrender and respite.

This week your provocation is the "Art of Trying Less." Try less to get the entire To-Do List finished; try less to be all things to all people; try less to do too much with too little time and energy; try less to cover your own greatness in order for others to be more comfortable around you. When you feel yourself using an effort that is draining you instead of empowering you, stop for a moment. Imagine that you can breathe slowly in and out through your heart. Do it until any feeling of "trying," of tightness, stagnancy, pressure, littleness, or tiredness begins to melt away. Then decide from the truest part of you if it is time for full, committed, decisive effort and action; *or* if it is time for true, happy basking, release, and respite. Choose one side or the other. Choose simply. Choose without guilt. Choose other than "trying." I think it was Yoda who said, "Try? There is no try. You either do or you don't do."

And as you choose this week keep remembering how beautiful and *good* you and your life are, no matter your current circumstances.

What if I were so busy
finding ways I could
uplift that I forgot to
rail against groups
and organizations
behaving badly?

Week 34

The Grandest Version of Ourselves

What if I were so filled up with my own passion, purpose, and genuine power that I didn't have time or interest in criticizing you or anyone else? What if the love and appreciation that I had flowing through me right now were so big and so constant that I could view everything and everyone with eyes of compassion, possibility, and wonder? What if I were so busy finding ways I could uplift that I forgot to rail against groups and organizations behaving badly? What if I decided to walk my own path so clearly and boldly that I *knew* everyone else could do it too? What if I practiced trusting that still small voice within so much that I felt the divine presence of well-being even while things seemed so fast and chaotic? And what if you did it too?

I think we can do it. I think it's actually possible. But somehow we learned to wait. Wait until we are more ready; wait until others tell us we are good enough; wait until people are nicer and the world is more ethical; wait until we graduate, get a different job, get married, get the house, retire, elect the right government officials. Mostly I think we are waiting around for everyone else to do it too. Or just someone. Anyone. To do what? To focus on being the grandest version of themselves that is possible in this very moment.

What do you think it would look like if a few of us started doing that right now? If we started *being*

What if
I practiced trusting
that still small voice within?

the grandest version of ourselves that we know to be? Right now with the imperfect, messy work situations, relationships, finances, and bodies that we have in this moment? Right now in the stressed-out, relief-seeking culture we live in? Right now when we don't have time to do anything more?

I want us to choose to do just that, to live the grandest version of ourselves that we can. Because I think amazing things will happen when we do. And we will laugh and love more. And we will start a ripple effect of good that can help heal the planet. And we will surprise ourselves with our own inner goodness and beauty.

If it feels too big and vague to say, "I'm going to start being the grandest version of myself that I can be," then here is a wonderful way to put it into motion. This is your provocation for the week. Choose a quality or essence that resonates with the grandest version of you that you can imagine. It might be love, strength, laughter, gentleness, discipline, patience, compassion, appreciation, persistence, joyfulness, honor, etc. There are many so just choose one that seems to be calling to you right now. Intend to embody that quality so fully that you experience it all week—within your thoughts, your feelings, your heart, and your actions. Each time you find yourself feeling tired, squished up, frustrated, drained, or "out of sorts" imagine this quality flooding through your entire being. Feel the essence of your grandest version as it begins to flow through your daily experiences.

The reason I know it's possible to begin living as our grandest selves is that I have experienced people practicing it. I have watched some of them, read their work, run into them at the store, listened to their music,

Be on the lookout for those who are practicing their grandest version.

and been inspired by their words or actions. I have been assisted by them and blessed by them in countless beautiful ways. And I believe with all of my heart that their ranks are growing. So this week be on the lookout for those who are practicing their grandest version; feel for them; hope to see them; expect to find them. And more importantly, let's choose in this moment to join them, to *be* them. Ah, the power of returning to our grandest version!

When something feels
difficult, unfair, or not
controllable by you,
first and foremost be
soft and nurturing
with yourself.

Week 35

Difficult Situations

Sometimes things happen that seem unfair or unethical. I have had people that I love, respect, and admire feel like this. It's hard to watch as their hearts are in pain—seemingly because of the actions of others. Have you ever had something like that happen? When you feel you don't have control over something that truly feels wrong to you? It could be behaviors of your own children, co-workers, parents, governments, banks, health-care systems, siblings, mentors, supervisors, spouses, clergy, etc. I had it happen once at a place I worked. Going through it feels gross.

But here is what I propose (again). Life is good and is always FOR us. Always. Even when it doesn't seem to be. This week's provocation is for when you are having difficulty with a situation that seems out of your control. You can use these tools to more gracefully move through a past situation as well. When something feels difficult, unfair, or not controllable by you, first and foremost be soft and nurturing with yourself. Truly, that is the first step. Then go through the three activities below and see if any resonate with you. If they do, use them gently.

Provocation #1: Before you fall asleep at night focus on the *feeling* that is *opposite* of the difficulty you are experiencing. For example, if you are watching a family member being hurtful to themselves or to someone else, try to get to the feeling of how good it feels when harmony, respect, and safe boundaries are practiced by the people you love. If someone at work or church is

Some of my most positive
and empowering changes
occurred directly as a result
of me making it through
what seemed like the most
difficult situations.

being unethical, practice the feeling of how wonderful it is to be around people you trust, who act with high levels of integrity. If your heart hurts because you are distant from someone you love, focus on how good it feels when you simply love and appreciate them. If someone has taken something from you, you could practice how much you love feeling safe and feeling like you have more than enough of everything you need to make life happy and fulfilling. It's not about the words; it's about getting to the *feeling that brings relief.* It takes energy and effort to get to the opposite feeling, but that's the important part.

Provocation #2: Take five or ten minutes to sit quietly and ask yourself, "Am I being called from somewhere within me to say something, take a stand, or otherwise try to change the situation here?" Gently notice what emerges when you ask yourself. No guilt. No pressure. Just ask.

Provocation #3: Ask yourself, "Is this an (or another) indication that it's time for me to move on, leave, or make some changes in my own life?" Again, just ask yourself and see what happens inside you. As with #2 give yourself some quiet time to listen within and reflect on whatever answers emerge.

If any of those three provocations call to you, go through the activity for a whole week. As things begin to shift—and they will—remember to be gentle and loving with you and with any others involved. Some of my most positive and empowering changes occurred directly as a result of me making it through what seemed like the most difficult situations. This week's provocations take courage and effort. Be gentle and kind with you as you play in them. We are such wonderfully bright, loving, and empowered beings. It

As things begin to shift—
and they will—remember
to be gentle and loving
with you and with
any others involved.

takes our intentions and our conscious choices to make it through difficult situations in such a way that we grow and gain goodness from them, instead of closing our hearts or being squished up by them. Your beautiful life is worth that. So is mine.

Imagine if we had
always been told that
we were inherently good
and deserved to be valued.

Week 36

Being Valued

I used to like listening to the CDs from Success Magazine. They were always full of really great stuff. I listened to one with a gentleman named Tony Schwartz as he talked about the importance of being valued—of *feeling* valued. He said that *feeling valued was as important to our emotional energy as sleep, nutrition, and exercise are to our physical energy.* Wow. I believe it. Most of us already know we need to sleep, eat, and move in order to be at our best. We may not always do it, but we know it. I don't think the same is true, however, for feeling valued.

Imagine what would happen if we got told over and over since we were kids, on the news, at school, from our parents, teachers, through health education, etc., that in order to feel and be *at our best* we needed to feel valued, loved, and appreciated. Imagine if we had always been told that we were inherently good and deserved to be valued. I bet we would take it more seriously and not think it was too soft and trivial to care about. And I think we would do things differently because we would really understand that being valued not only feels great, but it also lowers our stress levels, increases our energy, and adds to our well-being.

But what I really think would happen—*what I would want to have happen*—is this. We would begin to realize, just like with diet and exercise, that being valued is our own job; that we must be the ones to make the changes. I love when people value, love, and appreciate me and what I do! And I love when they let me know it. It feels great when that happens! But do you notice that

If we always wait for others'
positive reactions in order
to feel valued, we
simply will not be able
to feel our true value
in any lasting,
meaningful way.

some days you just aren't surrounded by family, friends, significant others, co-workers, teachers, supervisors, audiences, etc., who take the time, energy, and initiative to tell you how much they value you? It may sound a bit dramatic, but I think it verges on abusive to base our personal value only on what others say about us. If we always wait for others' positive reactions in order to feel valued, we simply will not be able to feel our true value in any lasting, meaningful way.

Here is your provocation for the week. On days when you aren't surrounded by people who tell you how much they value you, or on days when they do but you still can't feel it—then it's your job to create that feeling from within. One of the most magical, graceful, and powerful ways to feel valued, loved, and appreciated is to begin to consciously, intentionally, and willingly *take your own energy to value, love, and appreciate others.* Almost nothing compares with the radiant inner joy and strength I feel when I take moments—on purpose—to dwell on what I love and appreciate about people, things, and situations in my world. It is as simple and profound as this: *I feel my own sense of inner value grow when I take time to consciously appreciate and feel the value of others.* It really is a win-win situation.

This week when you notice that you have low energy or when you aren't feeling as loved or valued as you would want, find someone or something to value. Send them appreciation on purpose. Radiate out to them a feeling of how much you value them. Focus on what you love about them. And feel how your own inner awareness of being strong, competent, and valued increases.

Do you want to know something else really beautiful? The more you do that for yourself first, the more you will be surrounded by people who can feel your value, and often tell you about it. How cool!

It turns out that
when we use our
personal strengths. . .
we are happier.
Just that, simple and
straight forward.

Week 37

Strengths

I have taught a wonderful class called Stress & the Art of Happiness. It is based on a Harvard Medical School Special Report on Positive Psychology. One of the things that the report focused on was the use of our strengths and virtues. It turns out that when we use our personal strengths… we are happier. Just that, simple and straightforward. Isn't that cool? Do you ever notice though that sometimes the simple things feel so mundane that they don't seem very important? Almost like if it's not hard or complicated it must not be worth much. But the longer I live the more I am sure that it is the simple things, chosen moment by moment, that are the real and only difference between a mediocre life lived day by day in emotional sleepiness and status quo; or a life that we love—rich in aliveness, beauty, challenge, growth, strength, compassion, love, playfulness, appreciation, and all the other things that make us *want* to get up in the morning and move radiantly, purposefully into our day.

I was reminded by the Harvard researchers that one of those simple things, one of those little choices that can make all the difference in a day (or even in a life!) is the willingness and intention to use our personal strengths more often.

In line with that remembrance you have two provocations for the week. First, choose one of your favorite strengths and use it consciously several times this week. Here is a partial list of personal strengths to help get you thinking about some of your own

Ask gently,
"What strength am
I being called to use?"

wonderful qualities: creativity, gentleness, flexibility, curiosity, integrity, bravery, love, determination, kindness, spirituality, persistence, humor, appreciation of beauty, honor, open-mindedness, gratitude, loyalty, hope, leadership, organization, patience, teamwork, emotional intelligence, vitality, etc. Pick one that you like, one that comes through you easily, one that feels natural and normal for you to use. And simply be present with yourself and bask in *how you feel* as you use it.

Second—and this is the one that feels rich and deep to me—imagine that your heart, or your innermost sacred Self, or the still small voice, or your highest version of you, or your soul, or God, or your favorite spiritual guide or teacher, has been calling you to use a particular strength. Which one would it be? Just be quiet for a moment. Breathe. Now ask gently, "What strength am I being called to use?" Even if you feel like you are just making up an answer, what strength is wanting to move through you? Use it this week and notice how you feel as you do.

And just for fun, remember that according to Harvard researchers, whenever we use them we will be adding to our levels of happiness, life satisfaction, and general well-being. Not a bad way to spend some time!

Do not fight
anything
about yourself
this week.

Week 38

Exactly As I Am

What if today you let yourself be exactly as you are? With all of your weirdnesses and limitations; without working on changing anything; without wanting *you* to be different? The truth is, we have to be who we are anyway—because even if we are working on changing or growing we are still who we are in this moment. But I think in some ways we fight who we are almost every day.

I used to lead a wonderful stress-reduction meditation session right after I taught a high energy Zumba dance class. I dance with a *lot* of energy and am always bright red and really sweaty when I get done. I remember always wishing I could have showered and changed before the sessions so that I would enjoy the meditation time more. No big deal until I started realizing how often I am not okay with myself exactly as I am in each specific moment. I often want to be at least a bit different from what I am in some way. As I was dwelling on that at the beginning of one of my stress-reduction sessions, right on cue one of the class participants apologized in advance because she said she would probably cough. Someone else came in and explained with embarrassment that he might breathe heavy because of all the allergens in the air.

Individually none of these things seem important, but it got me thinking about how often we don't just allow ourselves to be exactly as we are right now in each moment. I love knowing we can expand and grow; I love knowing that our hearts' longings will always move us forward; I love knowing that we can make changes and

I think that might be a good definition of love—to look at something and simply accept it just as it is, without condition, without railing against it.

create lives we love. I focus on those things much of my time. But this week I am asking you to dwell on the other side of the coin. This week is about basking in the current "is-ness" of you—right now, exactly as you are in this moment.

Your provocation is extremely simple—as in easy to understand—but it's also extremely difficult to put into practice. Here it is: do not fight anything about yourself this week. Be fully present with however you are being, however you are acting, however you are feeling, and however you are thinking—and just *let yourself* be that way.

Sometimes you may be more tired than you want to be, or feel heavier, weaker, or less flexible than you want; sometimes you may feel older than you want to feel, or you may crave foods or drinks that you wish you didn't. But this week, however you show up, start with your body and say to it over and over, *"Today, I'm going to let you be exactly as you are."*

Sometimes you may be impatient with people you love, or even take them for granted; sometimes you may be less attentive or loving to them than you wish you would be; sometimes you may even be critical or judgmental with them. But this week I am asking you to look at how you show up in relationships (and provided that you are not being physically or emotionally abusive) say to yourself, *"Today, I'm going to let you be exactly as you are."*

Sometimes at home or work you may not get as much done as you would like, or maybe you work on little things instead of the bigger important ones; sometimes you may feel too overdone to do anything wholeheartedly; sometimes maybe you work more than you think you should. But this week decide to look at

Me, exactly as I am.
You, exactly as you are.
This week let's decide
it is already enough.

how you are at work and at home and say, *"Today, I'm going to let you be exactly as you are."*

I think that might be a good definition of love—to look at something and simply accept it just as it is, without condition, without railing against it. The cool irony is, when we soften enough to accept ourselves as we are right now—positive changes happen much more easily anyway. Me, exactly as I am. You, exactly as you are. This week let's decide it is already enough.

How I describe things
is generally the
way they continue
to show up.

Week 39

What's Your Story?

When you talk about the big areas of your life, what do you say? In terms of your health, money, relationships, personal/spiritual growth, time, work, and play what are the stories you tell about them? They don't feel like "stories." We experience them as facts. So asked another way, what are the facts you know to be true in regard to those big life areas?

Some of my story lines, or facts, feel good—life affirming and uplifting. In other areas my stories, that is to say my description of "how things are," are more limiting and don't feel so good.

That wouldn't be all that interesting except for this: notice that what you say about those areas and what you experience in those areas match really closely. *The stories I think, believe, and tell about my life match beautifully with how I experience my life… whether the stories are positive or negative.* Whether my stories say, "Relationships are hard" or "My relationships rock," "My body heals quickly" or "High blood pressure runs in my family," "There's not enough money to go around" or "Money has always been pretty easy to come by," I always end up "right." Meaning, *how I describe things* is generally the way *they continue to show up.*

The normal argument or logic says, "Well, of course that's my story. Things happened in my life to make me believe that's the way things are." But I think that's backwards. I think we pick up thoughts, beliefs, and habits of action (i.e. our "stories") from lots of places including our parents, teachers and coaches, church,

One of the most
powerful ways to
change our experience
is to change the
story first.

the news, friends, even social media, and then keep those ideas and expectations in motion creating more of what we are used to seeing. It's an unconscious cycle most of us don't even know we are participating in.

I'm not saying that our experiences aren't factual or real. Clearly they are. I just think that they are way more pliable than we realize. And one of the most powerful ways to change our experience is to change the story *first.* Easier said than done, but wildly important nonetheless. Here is your provocation for the week. Look honestly at the big areas: health, wealth, relationships, work/self-expression, time, personal/spiritual growth. Then go through your personal stories about each of them. Notice how clearly what you believe (i.e. your "story") and what you experience match. Now take one specific thing that you would like to experience more positively (for example a particular relationship, your work-life balance, how you pay your bills, what you eat, how you sleep, etc.) and begin to create a new story. The easiest way I have found to create a new, more beneficial story is to first *stop telling the life-crunching one.* No more complaining about it… to anyone.

Next, begin to tweak your facts, truths, and beliefs with a sincere attempt to see it the way you want it. Was there even one time that they didn't disappoint you? Is there even a small part of you that feels healthy or good today? Did you have the money any time this week to buy food and gas even if the prices are high? When you find even a *tiny* part of the story that matches the way you want it to be—hang on to it! Keep looking at it and keep telling that part of the story, to yourself and even to others. Pretend it's true that the stories you tell will out-picture (or begin to show up) in your real experiences. Choose to tell a new life-affirming story. Be aware of how you feel as you do, and then see what begins to manifest in your experiences. We are powerful beings—in a really, really good way!

What if you felt your breathing move in and out, and decided it is worthy of your attention?

Week 40

This Moment

What if this very moment were enough? What if it was already good enough to enjoy? What if you took the time, intention, and *choice* to notice it fully and even enjoy it? What might happen in your life if you did that once today—or twice—or twenty or more times, until it became a habit? My habit up until this point has often been different from that. I have become aware that I am almost always focusing on getting somewhere else. So often throughout my day I am trying to finish something, only so that I am able to move on to the next thing, in order to complete *it*, to move on to *something else*, to finish *it*… and on and on.

But what if right now, in this mundane moment as you are reading this—with perhaps not quite enough time, and with things not yet complete, and with the world as chaotic as it is, and with home and work and relationships and your body and your finances exactly as they are—what if you felt the chair underneath you, and felt your breathing move in and out through you, and simply *decided* that this moment is enough, that it is good, that it is worthy of your attention?

I imagine that when I am finally lying on my deathbed, perhaps looking over my life, if I am given a chance to come back to this very moment, I might think, "With all of its weirdness, chaos, or busyness, with all of its boredom or confusion, with all of its drama or lack of, with all of its success or disappointment—that particular moment was very, very good." Just because it was lived.

Consciously live
as many moments
as you can, and
decide that they
are enough. Because
quite simply they are.

Your provocation this week is to consciously live as many *moments* as you can, remembering to notice them, be here with them, breathe with them, and decide that they are enough. Because quite simply—they are.

Be loving and gentle with you this week and intend to enjoy your many moments, even the funky ones!

When we feel stressed or overdone it is, to a large degree, because our minds have been working overtime.

Week 41

Heart's Intelligence

I love the idea of the heart's intelligence because it assumes that there is something more expanded than our wonderful, bright minds only. Don't get me wrong. Our minds rock! I love to be able to think clearly and figure things out. I love to use my mind to create plans and then think about how to put them into practice. I love the fact that I can direct my powerful thoughts into any direction I choose. It's just that when we feel stressed or overdone it is, to a large degree, because our minds have been working overtime—planning, figuring, worrying, analyzing, thinking, always thinking—and still not coming up with the solutions to "fix" all the things that are troubling or overwhelming us. That's exhausting.

The heart, on the other hand, is where inspiration comes from; it is where the strength of the mind, the vulnerability of our emotions, and the goodness and divinity of our soul come together. It merges wisdom, love, and real power. Being open to the heart's intelligence is a way we can go beyond what is happening right now and reach toward solutions, processes, and perspectives that we could not see before. Using the heart's intelligence is a way to bring the magical, mystical, spiritual essence back into our experiences—even when things are still as busy, stressful, or challenging as they have been. What a beautiful possibility.

You can feel when you start to access your heart's intelligence because not only does the frantic "busyness" of the mind begin to slow down a bit, but the body reacts really beautifully as well. I can often feel a gentle

Ask your
heart for
guidance.

(and much needed) dropping of my shoulders and slight softening in my forehead and eyes. Then my breath moves back toward a slower, fuller, more healthful rhythm. The most wonderful thing I feel when I access my heart's knowing is the relief that comes with peacefulness and the joy that comes with appreciation—both at the same time! Here is one way to access your heart's intelligence and it is your provocation for the week. Intend to do it a few times a day and just feel what happens.

1. Bring your attention to the area of your heart, the same way you would if I said, "Notice your right hand." You can put your hand over your heart if that helps.
2. Imagine you could breathe in and out through your heart. Use long, slow breaths, about 4 counts in and 4 counts out. Stay with this step until you begin to feel a gentle slowing or softening.
3. Now bring your awareness to someone or something that matters a great deal to your heart. On purpose dwell for a few minutes on what specifically you like or love about them. His hilarious laugh or how he unconditionally loves or supports you? The way she hugs you, looks at you, or purrs on your lap? The majesty or infinite love you feel whenever you look at or think about a certain thing—perhaps someone's youth and friskiness, or maybe their deep wisdom, or the awesome beauty of a special place? It doesn't matter what or who you pick as long as it means a great deal to your heart.

It feels beautiful anytime you do this practice, but you can also use it if you need help solving a problem or if you want a new perspective on a challenging situation. Just do the above practice *first,* letting yourself get to

You may find yourself deeply grateful for the simplicity and power of your heart's intelligence.

that wonderful place of love or appreciation. Then, ask your heart for guidance. You may find yourself deeply grateful for the simplicity and power of your heart's (infinite) intelligence. I always am.

And if this provocation calls to you check out HeartMath Institute. I love those people and the work they do on the planet!

Create a few minutes
or hours to immerse
yourself in something
you enjoy.

Week 42

When Not on Vacation

I totally crack myself up. Do you ever notice that tiny little shifts in perspective can make a huge difference? It happened to me the other day when I was remembering how I used to come down to Sarasota, Florida every 3-4 months to visit my mom. While she would go to work I would slather up sunscreen, go to the beach, and sit there for a few hours every day. I love it so much when I close my eyes and listen to the waves lap up on the beach and feel the wind on me. It's delicious. Mostly I would go by myself and do the things I love to do: listen, feel, meditate, talk to God, write, nap, and plan/create/visualize my grandest version of me living in Florida and being a New York Times best-selling author and speaker. Ahh…

I am still working toward those goals. I live in Florida now (woo hoo!), but here's the crack up. I realized that I had hardly been going to the beach, or even taking any time off to play, relax, go somewhere fun with Nikolas or friends, or just do "nothing." Because on the weekends, and when I would get off work, and when I would take vacation time I was so intent on writing, editing, updating my speaker's packet, researching, etc., to move forward with my lifework stuff that I was not giving myself the emotional space or permission to just stop all kinds of working.

I remember one Saturday when Nik went over to our wonderful friends' house to play with their dogs, swim, and just have some fun. I had a few hours to myself and I felt myself immediately and happily start planning: edit a chapter in my book, work on a rough

Because you are
radiant even if it feels
like that has been
covered up for awhile.

draft of my new speaker's brochure, clean the house, change the sheets and do laundry, water the flowers, create something beautiful for dinner. I love having those things all accomplished. I even love *doing* them when I give myself lots of time. But when I plan, or want to accomplish, so many good things that I cannot do them all it stops being fun and starts feeling like a "hamster wheel." So in the middle of trying to decide which of these good things to work on first, I got one of those crystal clear inner messages that told me to go to the beach. Hmm… that was not in the plan.

I went to the beach. I stayed for a few hours listening, feeling, meditating, half napping, and visioning/visualizing my amazing life. It was simply beautiful on all levels. And then with what seemed almost no effort at all I came home and played in many of the other things I had wanted to do. Not all of them, but many. And it happened with a relaxed, easy, playful sort of feeling that lasted all day.

There is something powerful about taking hours or even minutes of "vacation"—even when we are not on vacation—that can shift our perspective and serve us so beautifully. So that is your provocation for the week. Whether it is the beach, the bookstore, the zoo, time with the kids or grandkids, a pet shop, time away from everyone, a massage, a garden, a fishing trip, an uninterrupted game, a good book, a creative project, the comfort of your own bed, or anything else that calls to you—create a few minutes or hours to immerse yourself in something you enjoy, in something you love to do that breathes life into you, inspires or refreshes you, and reminds you of your radiance. Because you *are* radiant… even if it feels like that has been covered up for awhile.

Just find something
and do it.
And then
keep doing it.

Week 43

One Little Choice

I often think about how glad I am to know *beyond a shadow of a doubt* that change is possible. Not always easy. Rarely easy, as a matter of fact. But always possible. I have been playing around with this consciousness "stuff" for a long time now, over two decades. I am getting clearer and clearer about something. It's not when the change is coming the easiest that the real transformation happens. Instead, it's when you want to give up, or cave, or forget it all, or start again tomorrow that the real possibility opens up to step into strength and real power to make changes.

I used to do a wonderful healing art form called Chi-Lel Qigong and it's a good example of what I'm talking about. When I learned the mind-body practice from Master Luke Chan, who I was told brought the form to the U.S. from China, we were instructed to do it for 100 consecutive days—which constituted one "gong" or level of practice. During our training everyone kept saying things like, "Well, if I miss day 49 then couldn't I just add a day to the end of the 100 days to make up for it?" And I remember him finally saying something like, "You Americans are so funny. You always jump from one thing to another trying to find a quicker, easier way. Just find something and do it. And then keep doing it."

Some days it felt easy and good to do the 16-minute movement form. However, the real success came on the days when I *so* didn't want to do it because I was too tired or too busy—but I did it anyway. I think the same is true for all the times we try to make changes.

I'm all about effortless and easy. I *love* when changes feel fun and easy to do. But I know it's when I am on

Ask for the courage and strength within to make one little choice that serves you well!

the border of, "Maybe today I'll choose to do what is truly better for me," or "Maybe not. Maybe I'll just do it tomorrow instead," that the real possibility of power and change are present. Whether with food or exercise decisions, actions within my relationships, consistency around disciplining my thoughts, steps toward expanding my career, or choices with financial habits, it always seems easy for a while to do something new and thus to *begin* the change. *But when the freshness and inspiration start to lessen and it feels like my good is still a long way off*—whether that's the completion of a 100-day Qigong practice, desired weight loss, increased wealth, or the success of a new book—when those things still seem to be a long way off and when I'm not in the mood to stick with the change today, *that is when one little choice—to do the highest and best for myself just in this moment—really matters!*

So that is your provocation for the week. If you have been wanting to make a positive change, if you have tried and failed, if you are currently in the process of making a change and are losing steam, or if you have almost decided to just forget it—each day this week decide on *one* small choice that you can make that serves you well. Maybe it's writing just one paragraph of your book, or taking the effort to go to the bank to put only $5 into a savings account, or being kind instead of impatient just one extra time with your spouse or child, or taking even a brief walk, or not eating the extra dessert just today. Feel the power in that moment, in that possibility, in that space that resides between the decision to do it or not do it.

And then ask for the courage and strength within to make that one little choice that serves you well! You are wonderfully worthy of a life of great good. We all are. Small choice by small choice we can get there.

You are allowed
to feel better in
this very moment.

Week 44

Pushing Against or Drawing Toward

I was reminded of the difference in my life when I push against what I *don't* want versus when I focus on what I *do* want. I still have days when there are more things for me to do than the time to do them. And they're all things I want to get done. When I focus on my perceived time shortage—which is what I *don't* want—I get tight in the shoulders and feel hurried, urgent, and annoyed with things. Sometimes it feels like I have a bee hive on my head—like everything is too fast and buzzing around too close. I know that sounds weird, but that's what it feels like when my mind has been working overtime for too long trying to figure everything out quickly.

Obviously when I feel like that I'm not in a place of ease and grace and intentional living—which is what I *do* want. It's only when I'm in that easy place feeling open, clear, and fully present that things get done for me *much* more gracefully, happily, and competently.

That awareness helps me remember a really simple but important difference: pushing against what I don't want makes more of what I don't want; looking toward what I do want creates more of what I do want. Notice how you feel as you read the following statements: "I don't like to be hurried; I don't want to be behind; I don't want my body to feel tight and constricted; I don't want to run out of time; I don't want more work than I can comfortably get done; I don't like to feel stressed." Yuck.

Focus consciously on what you do want.

The harder I push on it the bigger it gets. Do you ever feel yourself pushing against what you *aren't* wanting?

This week decide instead to remember the wonderful tool of focusing on or looking toward what you *do* want, *even if it is not yet here.* If I do that with my example, my thoughts can change into: "I love the way I feel when I get things done well; I love having plenty of time; I love listening to my body's messages and following those messages; I love to feel happy; I love having soft, relaxed shoulders; I love that I am competent and can do lots of good things; I love doing my life work in such beautiful ways; I love when things feel effortless and easy; I love to remember that there is a rhythm and flow to all things so if I feel fast and busy right now, a slower time of respite will come around soon; I love that I am in charge of my thoughts." I simply feel better—happier, more fulfilled, more at peace—every moment of the day when I take my mental discipline to do that—*to look toward and focus on what I do want, instead of pushing against what I don't want.*

You are allowed to feel better in this very moment. Invite yourself to do so by using this week's provocation. Instead of pushing against what is difficult, what is challenging, what you are not wanting, focus consciously on what you do want. Play with it in new thoughts, words, sentences, visuals, or actions until you *feel* a shift toward lightness and ease. Relief really can happen in any moment that you choose to shift. Just try and see what happens!

When I confuse
the wonderful urge
toward growth and expansion
with the need or
desire to be perfect
it's exhausting.

Week 45

When Imperfection is Good Enough

I'm currently in my early fifties. I have been practicing this self-care "stuff" since my twenties in one way or another. Yet I realized this weekend that sometimes I am still trying to be perfect… or at least wanting to be perfect… or more accurately, wanting things in my world to be perfect. It even sounds ridiculous when I write it, but it's true. The house, my body, my projects, my speaking, my writing, my finances, my relationships, my spiritual connection, my inner growth—I love it when they are all working wonderfully, just the way I want them to. I do. Perhaps more truthfully, I love it when *I am doing what I need to do* so that things are working wonderfully. I think there is something expansive and healthy in that. It's so important to know what makes my heart sing, and then to work toward it. However, when I confuse the wonderful urge toward growth and expansion with the need or desire to be perfect—it's exhausting. It's also abusive.

It seems that for some people "good enough" really is good enough. But for so many of us, things are not "good enough" until they are perfect. It's as if we have made a habit out of trying to make everything "perfect enough" *on the outside* so that we can finally feel relief, or be proud of ourselves, or experience peace, or relax, or feel content, or empowered, or strong, or happy—*on the inside.*

The problem is I have noticed that when we are try-

Anytime we move to
the point of being
overwhelmed or overdone,
we are not taking
care of ourselves.

ing so hard to be "perfect"—in order to then feel better or happier in some way—we often stop taking care of ourselves. Anytime we go past our point of ease, anytime we move to the point of being overwhelmed or overdone, we are not taking care of ourselves. And just as a reminder because at some level of your being you already know this: *You cannot feel truly good about yourself or enjoy your life if you are not first taking good care of yourself. Nor can you take good care of others if you don't take good care of yourself first.* For me that means going to sleep when I am tired, even when company is here and my house doesn't look perfect; spending time with my son even before my To-Do List is finished; being gentle and easy with me even when I think back over my day and find I was way less "perfect" than I would have liked to have been, and on and on.

In the spirit of letting "perfection" take a break this week, here is your provocation. Do these two things simultaneously over the next 7 days and just see what happens. First, intend to do your very best—working or playing toward your highest good or your greatest vision at home, at work, wherever you are—because it simply feels wonderful and empowering to do that. And second, *decide* to give yourself a break when you fall short of whatever you have deemed "perfection." It really is a decision you can make. And I am pretty sure that any human version of "perfection" is a myth anyway—unless we define it as "things exactly as they already are." I know it's hard to swallow, but what if everything is already in Divine Order, and what if each one of us is already a precious part of that Divine Order?

How does
happy show up
for you?

Week 46

Happily Adding Value

I was wondering what our days would look like if we remembered every morning that being happy was a good intention. I am not talking about a "fakey-sugary-sweet-pretending-to-smile-when-we're-having-a-crappy-day" happy. I'm talking about the inner permission and the actual *choice* to pick thoughts, words, and actions that move us in the direction of increasing our happiness and well-being. Sometimes my "happy" feels alive and childlike and playful; sometimes it feels spiritual and sacred and full; sometimes it feels deep and peaceful and restful; sometimes my "happy" feels empowered, on purpose, and inspired to be the greatest version of me that I can be; sometimes it even feels soft and melancholy which can help me slow down and release for a bit. How does happy show up for you?

Experiencing happiness, no matter which way it shows up, is obviously a beautiful thing. The only problem is, it's one thing to know we want to be happy, but it's quite another thing to find practical ways to move toward greater happiness, especially when life feels so fast and busy most of the time. As I was dwelling on that, I heard John Maxwell, a leadership expert, talk about a practice that he likes to participate in. He said to start each day asking the question, "Who can I add value to today; and how can I do it?" I love that! As I listened to his words and felt the energy of that message move through me, I realized how perfect it was not only as a way to assist others and to be a great leader, but also as a way to bring great meaning and happiness to our own daily experience as well. Talk about a win-win situation!

Every person on the planet benefits when even one of us moves closer to living our highest good.

There is something about helping another person that brings out our own strength and value; it causes us to find a reservoir of well-being within us from which to act. If I ask how I can add value to someone else's life, there is implicit knowing in that question that I myself have value! And that knowing helps to fuel a beautiful cycle: when I live from the understanding that I have great value, I step toward choices that move me toward fulfilling or living my highest good, my highest intentions, my highest visions and goals. So I get happier *and* all the people around me benefit too, because I think that every person on the planet benefits—or has value added to their life—when even *one* of us moves a single step closer to living our highest good.

So here is your provocation for the week. Ask yourself, "Who can I add value to today; and how can I do it?" Take a few minutes to breathe into that question. Then notice the wonderfully uplifting, empowering cycle that happens when your actions and choices—mental, emotional, and physical—are in alignment with that. Ahhh…

Thanks, John Maxwell!

Now, of course
we are each already
good enough exactly
as we are. Period.

Week 47

Your Personal Priority List

What does your list look like? Not your incessant every day To-Do List that tells you in a critical way what you "should" be doing, but your Personal Priority List (PPL) that tells you what you would need to do in order to be impeccable with yourself, to live the highest version of you that you are called to live, and to be truly proud of yourself. Now, of course we are each already good enough exactly as we are. Period. At the same time, there is an essence within each person continually urging, moving, pushing us to go forward, to create and experience more good—for ourselves, for those we love, for the whole planet. I have heard it called the feeling of Divine Discontent. It's that part of us that says, "You are good. You are worthy. You can do *anything.* What *will* you do?"

My list sounds too big to me sometimes. Yet they are all things I feel sure about. They are things that when I move toward them—not perfectly, but *toward* them—my life is infinitely enhanced. I am happier. I am more proud of myself. I am more effective in the world. I am a grander version of me than when I don't.

I think it's easy for us to try to turn our list into a "should" list, to let guilt move in and have an all-or-nothing attitude. I think sometimes I don't let myself be aware of my PPL because I know I'm not going to do everything on it right now. And I think I'm secretly afraid that maybe I'll never do some of them—and that makes me sad or frustrated or disappointed. But today I'm calling all of us to look at our own PPL anyway. You can find yours by answering this question: What

You are good.
You are worthy.
You can do anything.
What will you do?

things would I need to do (or not do!) in order to be impeccable with myself and to live the highest version of me that I am called to live?

Today is about being courageous, being inspired, being *awakened* by your PPL. Guilt puts you to sleep; simple awareness awakens your greatness!

Your provocation this week is to write your list somewhere. And look at it. And celebrate that it calls to you! Then move—*even if only so slightly*—toward at least one of the things on your list. Or celebrate at least one of the things that you are already doing impeccably.

Here is my PPL today. I purposely wrote them in the present tense. Some I already do consistently; some I don't; some I do on and off:

I meditate and pray every day, listening for the still small voice within me and taking action on the beautiful inner guidance I receive.

I walk, run, or dance 45-60 minutes ~4 days a week, enjoy 20-60 minutes of yoga ~3 times a week, and do strength training 2-3 days a week.

I eat "clean" foods (mostly veggies, fruits, beans, nuts, fish, or happily raised chicken, and a few whole grains), drink ~75 ounces of water a day, enjoy food through dinner, and then let my body fast until morning.

I replace any sugar cravings with a gentle mindfulness as I simply watch the craving instead of immediately acting on it.

I consistently save at least 10% of all my income, continually learn about and work toward financial freedom, and go on at least 2 fun vacations or adventures a year.

I work ~10 hours a week on my author/speaker career—writing, editing, sending out books and brochures, following up with radio interviewers, event planners/coordinators, and playing in my website.

Guilt puts you to sleep;
simple awareness
awakens your
greatness!

Daily I spend some quality time being totally present with Nikolas, Mom, and Chris.

I write down 3 specific, different things I am grateful for each day.

I begin and end my day reading out loud and attempting to *feel* my vision statement and my most important life goals as if already completed.

I am gentle and compassionate with myself and others, and I intentionally look for the strength, goodness, and infinite possibilities in people even if they are not feeling it or showing it.

I sleep ~8 hours each night and feel fully rested and energized most every morning.

It's bizarre and annoying and wonderful how many things can call to us! Play in your own Personal Priority List this week and let it inspire you and bring you relief and joy.

I think we work
way too hard mentally.

Week 48

Breathe in Your Good

I love to walk. Often my walks turn into wonderful meditations where thoughts, insights, feelings, spiritual connection, and intuitive metaphors all sort of come together. I still remember a beautiful visual that came to me one evening when I was walking some time ago. It was a God thing, I am sure of that. It's as powerful and good for me now each time I remember it as it was that evening.

I had been thinking about how hard I work—how hard we all work—at the changes we want. Sometimes we work hard at the action steps—maybe not consistently or gracefully, but we do work "hard." More often, however, I think we work way too hard mentally—at least I have—by consistently worrying about or pushing against whatever I want to be different. It could be changes with my body, relationships, spiritual connection, money, career, or how I experience time. I was thinking about how much energy I put out—either through goal oriented actions or through my mind's constant "busyness" going over and over the challenge (or opportunity). My mind's constant activity often looks like: planning, creating, worrying, getting excited, feeling strong one moment then doubtful the next, feeling an urgency to create the changes one day but tired and mentally lazy another day.

The truth is the exciting, satisfying, and often difficult process of changing thoughts and actions in order to create something new, something grander, something that serves the highest good to an even greater degree, takes a lot of effort mentally, emotionally,

Feel the simplicity,
the power, and the
ease of breathing
in your good.

and spiritually. It can take a toll on us at every level of our being if we don't balance it with being satisfied in this very moment.

Is it just me, or do you notice sometimes there are things that you are working on consciously by attempting new thought patterns and/or new actions… but also working on by default because even when you aren't working on it you are still worrying about it, analyzing it, or criticizing yourself for not working on it? I still do that sometimes and it's exhausting. Really.

While I had been walking that evening I had been thinking about how often I do that. I wasn't even feeling critical of myself about it. I was just sort of able to see it, to see that it was sometimes my pattern. I remember feeling compassion for myself because I could see how tired it makes me. And that's when I got this beautiful visual that felt like a blessing from higher guidance. It was simply to "Breathe in your good." I saw me just breathing in, and watching and feeling all my good moving toward and into me. I felt the simplicity and the "rightness" of it then and each time I remember it. It always makes my shoulders soften and go down. And if I have been feeling urgent or impatient with myself for not moving faster with books or other projects, remembering that visual always softens me and brings lightness and relief, and sometimes tears.

Feel the simplicity, the power, and the ease of breathing in your good. No effort, no struggle, no time line. Feel your body soften as you imagine simply breathing in whatever you truly want so that it just moves effortlessly into your experience. Breathe in a lean, healthy body. Breathe in love and intimacy into your relationships. Breathe in having enough money. Breathe in spiritual connection. Breathe in meaning and purpose through your work and play. Breathe in happiness and appreciation for yourself and for your life.

Know you are worthy.
Know you are loved.
Know you have
great value.

Your provocation this week is just that. Create the visual of breathing in your good. Then choose to bask, just for a few moments, in the possibility that it can be easy, simple, and that good. Relax. Soften. Know you are worthy. Know you are loved. Know you have great value. And just breathe in your good. I love the magical, powerful presence of ease and relief.

I think we came
to this planet to
remember who
we really are
and to embody
our highest selves.

Week 49

Right Thought, Right Action

I think we came to this planet to remember who we really are and to embody our highest selves. I think we came to experience our greatest good, our highest love, and our most magnificent purpose and potential! And I think we need to work toward self-mastery in order to do that. For me, self-mastery is the awesome power to look within myself, take personal responsibility for all of my experiences, choose to make peace with whatever is showing up in that moment, and then... *move intentionally forward by consistently doing whatever is needed to move me in the direction of my soul's highest dreams.* I think we are all being called to do that.

In order to practice self-mastery there are two concepts we need to balance: Right Thought *and* Right Action. The key word is "and." If we don't do *both* I don't think we can experience the fulfillment, the power, or the grace that self-mastery can bring.

I know... because I've often only played in one or the other.

I've done a lot of Right Thought. That's when you work on changing your thoughts, feelings, and mental images to match what it is that you want—instead of seeing only what is currently true. It takes a lot of mental discipline and involves meditation, prayer, "acting as if" (practicing that things are the way you want them to be), visualizing, doing affirmations, and engaging in positive self-talk. Some of the most important concepts

Work on changing your thoughts, feelings, and mental images to match what it is that you want.

I've found for strengthening my own Right Thought are: the Law of Attraction, New Thought spirituality, the process of co-creating, taking 100% responsibility for everything that shows up in my world, understanding the concept of self-fulfilling prophecy, the power of visualization, the principles of success, and how thoughts can affect feelings. For me, Right Thought also has much to do with asking for Divine guidance and assistance, using my intuition, strengthening my spiritual connection, and trusting God or the Universal Essence. I have practiced Right Thought often over the years and at times it serves me well.

I've also done a lot of Right Action. That's when you take specific action steps toward what you want to experience or accomplish. There have been many times in my life where I have worked hard by outlining a goal, planning action steps, proceeding forward (either gracefully or with lots of "pushing"), and then checking things off my To-Do List. I can get a really good hamster wheel of action going! It's how I often made my way through school, and is sometimes the way I have gotten other projects completed too. I love my ability to utilize Right Action and at times, it too has served me well.

But here's the catch. I have usually done one or the other—*either* worked on trying to think and feel differently or moved forward with action steps or behaviors. I have not yet made a consistent habit out of the graceful integration of doing both: Right Thought *with* Right Action—which from my perspective is the only way miraculous, meaningful, fulfilling transformations can gracefully and consistently occur.

Do you know anyone who stays on the Right Thought side but who is not doing any actions to back it up? "I know things will change. I'm visualizing it.

Move with intensity
and passion into the pragmatic
and specific Right Actions
that you are inspired
to take!

I'm praying about it. I feel it. I'm meditating on it." Yet things are not changing for them. It's comical really, though I can't make too much fun because I have been there myself! And do you know anyone who is more comfortable with the Right Action side? It's all about "git 'er done!" but by the end of the project we often look and feel beaten up or overdone, and have results not nearly as big as the effort we put forth. I'm familiar with that one too!

So… your provocation this week is to engage in both. As you work with whatever is "on your plate" this week, always *begin* with Right Thought by visualizing or thinking about your goal *as if it's already completed.* Yes, it takes mental/emotional effort to do this, but believe me it's worth it. Work to be able to *feel* powerful and renewing emotions like inspiration, appreciation, gratitude, or love. And *then* move with intensity and passion into the pragmatic and specific Right Actions that you are inspired to take! What a brilliant combination!

So many simple moments
can become beautiful.

Week 50

Love or a Call for Love?

What if everything you experience is one of two things: either love or a call for love? Really… everything. I heard the concept for the first time years ago when my mom had read it in a book by Marianne Williamson. As I was remembering the concept I had some interesting and beautiful experiences because of it. When deciding which category things go in—either Love or a Call for Love—it's pretty easy when they feel either "good" or "bad." Nikolas laughing so hard at the table that he can't stop (often until I can't help myself and start laughing too)? Easy—Love. The guy in the car beside me looking really mad and blowing his horn because the driver in front of him didn't go through the light quickly enough? Easy—Call for Love.

What was really surprising, though, was when I did it with the things that seemed mundane, neutral, or unimportant. I challenged myself to do this provocation and literally put *everything* I experienced into one of those two categories. It's amazing to me that when I go through my day that way there are so many opportunities to feel peaceful, full, and happy. So many simple moments can become beautiful. Walking through the parking lot seeing and hearing some acorns drop onto the parked cars—Love. Passing people in the hall—Love. Feeling tired—Call for Love. Taking a big drink of water—Love. Hearing bits of the news—Call for Love. Me being annoyed that the television was turned up loud when I came into the fitness center—Call for Love. The person enjoying the TV—Love.

Imagine sending that person, situation, or even yourself love, compassion, healing energy, and the simple intentions of well-being.

Your provocation this week is simple. Pretend it is true that *everything* you see, hear, and experience today and all week is either Love or a Call for Love. Even if your wonderful, linear, logical, rational mind says you do not know what category it should be in, do it anyway. Put everything this week into either the Love pile or the Call for Love pile. If it is Love, let yourself bask for a few moments in the fullness and goodness of it. I have been surprised at how many—so very many—beautiful moments there are. And when you find something that is a Call for Love, imagine sending that person, situation, or even yourself: love, compassion, healing energy, and the simple intention of well-being.

Me getting to write this—Love.

Mundane or magnificent
it matters not, just focus
for a moment on
what you want.

Week 51

You Get What You Look For

This is one of those concepts that sounds so simple or mundane that you might think it doesn't have much power to affect you. From the bottom of my very full heart, though, I ask that you put this week's provocation into practice in the most intentional way you can. Because out of it can come huge beneficial changes for you, for me, for anyone who plays in it. I am sure of that.

What is it that you want? As specific or general as you want to be, what do you really want right now? A pain-free body? The ability to sleep soundly and wake up rested and energized? Healing and forgiveness between you and a family member? A breath of hope that things can get better? A successfully completed creative project? A loving, meaningful relationship? Enough money to live comfortably? Greater spiritual connection? Work that you love? The disappearance of a long-held addiction or negative habit? You at a healthy weight? To be excited and passionate about your life? The time to do what you want to do? The ability to love and approve of yourself? Ease and relief? A specific car, house, or vacation? Mundane or magnificent it matters not, just focus for a moment on what you want.

Now, *start looking for examples of it.* Be willing to look for the slightest nugget that matches what you want. Look for it within your own past experiences or within someone else's belief that it is possible. Look for

What happens when
we start to look for
what we want is
quite simply this:
we begin to see
examples of it.

it by creating visualizations, mental images, or positive thoughts about it. Look for any book, speaker, TV show, blog, article, movie, app, or YouTube clip that matches the essence of what you want. Start looking for people talking about it in line at the grocery store or at your kid's soccer game. Not the ones discussing the lack of it, but instead look for and focus on the stories, programs, or people who are already creating, living with, expecting, or enjoying the same thing you want.

What happens when we start to look for what we want is quite simply this: we begin to see examples of it. It really is quite amazing. First you may see just small examples, or it will be other people experiencing it so it still seems far away. But if you keep it up, if you keep looking for what you want, examples will come more often; they will start getting bigger, coming closer, and getting more real. It's almost miraculous, but you have to begin the process by taking the effort (and it is effort) to look for examples of what you want—before you have it!

Here is your provocation for the week. It's a fun one. If you do it, it can be like a wonderful experiment. First, choose to assume or pretend it's true that you get what you look for. Second, pick one thing that would make you happy to have added, expanded, or gotten rid of in your life. Third, every day this week find at least one example of this good thing. Even if it feels like you are stretching to come up with examples, keep looking each day until you find at least one thing that matches what you want. If you have diligently looked and found no examples in the day, then simply create an example or picture of it within your own mind's eye or mental image before you go to bed. Be your own researcher. Keep it up for a whole week and watch what starts to be drawn to you. I love the way life works!

You care about this kind of
self-care "stuff" and because
of that you literally shift
the energies of this planet
and help make it
a better place.

Week 52

The Magic of Gratitude

According to Positive Psychology researchers there are some consistent things that not only lower our stress, but also make us feel happier (both short-term and long-term), if we choose to play in them. One of those things is practicing the feeling of gratitude. I doubt many would argue with that. It totally makes sense. And it turns out we don't have to wait for gratitude or appreciation to "come upon us" so to speak. Instead, we can conjure the feeling intentionally.

Now, it is one thing to understand conceptually that gratitude is a good thing. It's quite another, however, to take the time and intentional effort needed to create the real feeling within. It's not just a mind thing, but for me it starts out a mental activity as I begin to think about something or someone I appreciate. The real magic happens, though, when my heart begins to open and I *feel* gratitude. There's a saying, "The longest journey a person must take is the eighteen inches from head to heart." I believe it. One of the easiest ways for me to get there—to *feel* great big gratitude—is to write a letter to someone and tell them all the things I appreciate or love about them. So I have decided to write you, my reader, a letter. While I did it I tried to feel for your individual energies as well as your energy as a readership whole!

Dear *You* reading this,

Thank you! I bet you didn't know it but there are things that you have done and ways that you are that have added great value to my life. And I appreciate you

Choose someone in your life and write them a letter of gratitude or appreciation.

deeply because of it. You care about this kind of self-care "stuff" and because of that you literally shift the energies of this planet and help make it a better place. How cool is that?!

And more personal for me, as I wrote these weekly provocations I always knew that there was the possibility of you being there—by Divine appointment I like to think—to eventually read them, so you helped make my writing come to life. Without that possibility my "Blurbs," as I like to call them, wouldn't have been as real or alive as I would have wanted. That may not seem like a big deal to you, but for me it's huge. You see, every day it is my intention to be an uplifting presence in some way. Writing is one of the ways I am called to do that. However, I don't think I can really do that—be beneficial or uplifting—unless I am authentic, unless I have the courage to be real.

As I wrote these, even before the words were completed and published, I liked to try to feel you around me. It may sound odd, but it never felt like I was writing to a blank screen. So you see, you have helped keep me present and open and real. You gave me a place and a reason to do that which I love to do. And you have inspired me to live my highest version of myself. You have encouraged me to remember what is good in life and reminded me to focus on that. And you have made me a better person by simply being present and being you. And that is a beautiful thing!

For those reasons and more, I love and appreciate who you are. So thank you—truly. My hope is that as you read this you will actually feel my gratitude move through you in a big way, and that you will just suck it all in and be wonderfully blessed by it! Because you deserve to feel loved, honored, and appreciated for the magnificent being that you are! Indeed—thank you.

Because you deserve to
feel loved, honored,
and appreciated for the
magnificent being
that you are!

And here is your final provocation. Choose someone in your life and write them a letter of gratitude or appreciation this week. You can give it to them if you want, but you don't have to in order to get all the delicious benefits of it. That means that pets and loved ones no longer with you are fair game too. And if you care what the Positive Psychology researchers have to say—the increase in our happiness levels when we do this beautiful little exercise can last for a *whole month!* Truly awesome!

About the Author

Dr. Darcy Lord received her Ph.D. from The Ohio State University in Somatic Education which addresses the mind-body-spirit connection. For over 25 years she has been a speaker and trainer in the areas of stress-reduction, empowerment, and self-care.

Along with speaking and writing about stress-reduction, happiness, practical spirituality, and personal empowerment, some of Dr. Lord's favorite things are spending time with her wonderful family and friends; meditating and playing in her own personal/spiritual growth; working out; dancing; and basking beside or in the Gulf of Mexico!

Dr. Lord's vision is to experience her own joy and divine alignment enough to help uplift the consciousness of the planet as a best-selling author and speaker continually calling people back to their own highest good. She and her son live in beautiful Venice, Florida.

CPSIA information can be obtained
at www.ICGtesting.com
Printed in the USA
LVHW021702220721
693399LV00010B/614